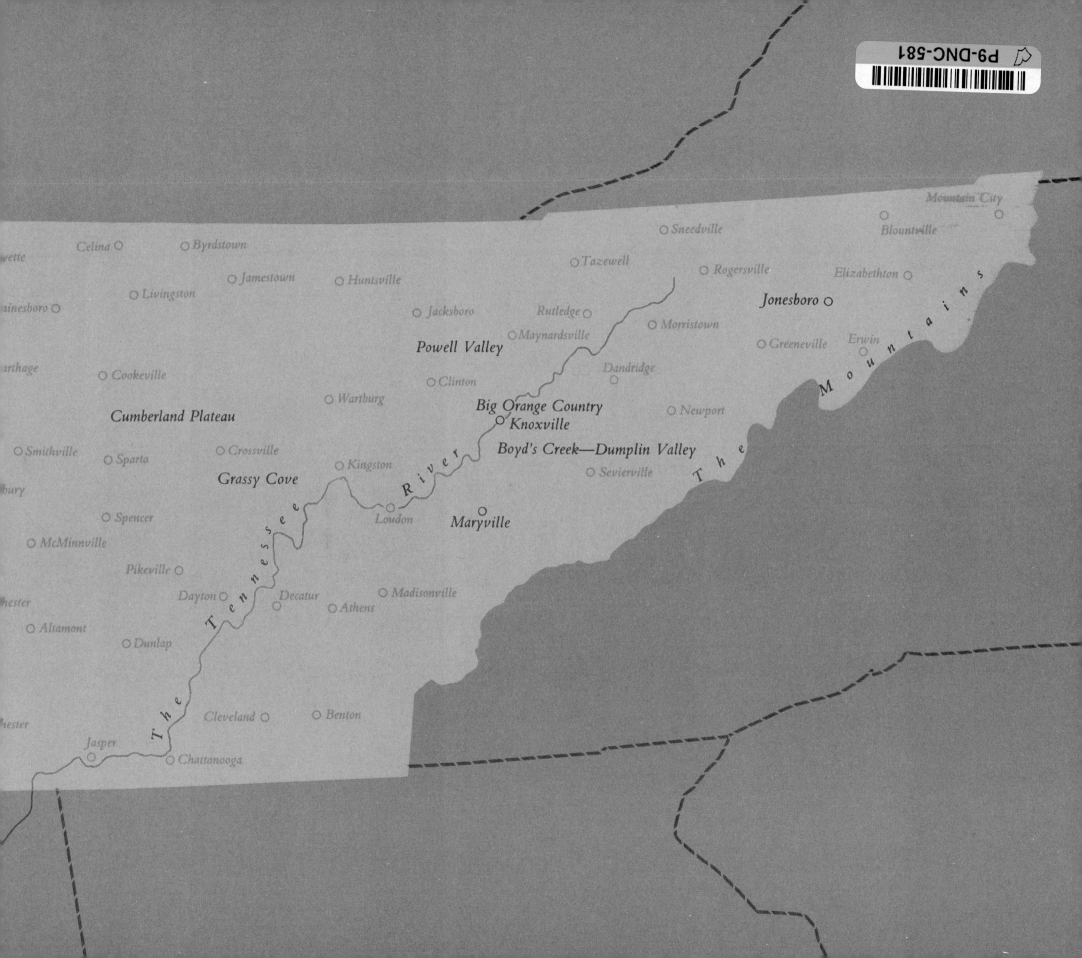

The Tennesseans

A PEOPLE AND THEIR LAND

For Rosemary Courtney —
Lamar Alexander

The Tennesseans

A PEOPLE AND THEIR LAND

Presented by Lamar Alexander
Photographed by Robin Hood
Text by Barry Parker

Thomas Nelson Publishers
Nashville

Published in Nashville, Tennessee,
by Thomas Nelson, Inc., Publishers
and distributed in Canada by
Lawson Falle, Ltd., Cambridge, Ontario.

Printed in the United States of America.

All royalties, after expenses, from the sale
of *The Tennesseans: A People and Their Land*
will go to a fund which Governor Alexander
has created to support scholarships and
awards for Tennessee's most outstanding
young musicians.

Dark as a Dungeon, by Merle Travis,
reprinted on p. 44, copyright © 1947 by Elvis Presley
Music & Unichappell Music, Inc. Copyright renewed.
Copyright © 1956 by Elvis Presley Music &
Unichappell Music, Inc. Rights controlled by Unichappell Music, Inc.
(Rightsong Music, Publisher). International coyright secured.
ALL RIGHTS RESERVED. Used by Permission.

Excerpt from "The Negro Speaks of Rivers," reprinted on
p. 172, from Langston Hughes, *Selected Poems of Langston Hughes,*
copyright © 1926, 1932 by Alfred A. Knopf, Inc.
Used by permission.

Typesetting by Bailey Typography Incorporated, Nashville, Tennessee.
Color separations by Graphic Process Incorporated, Nashville, Tennessee.
Text paper 100# Lustro Offset Enamel Dull
supplied by Clements Paper, Nashville, Tennessee.
Printing by American Printers & Lithographers, Chicago, Illinois.
Binding material Holliston Sail Cloth supplied by
The Holliston Mills Incorporated, New Canton, Tennessee.
Binding by Nicholstone Book Bindery, Nashville, Tennessee.

Library of Congress Cataloging—in Publication Data

Main entry under title: The Tennesseans.

   Summary: Presents many aspects of the varied
land and people of Tennessee.
   1. Tennessee—History, Local. [1. Tennessee]
I. Alexander, Lamar.   II. Hood, Robin, ill.
III. Parker, Barry.
F436.T257 1981   976.8   81-9597
ISBN 0-8407-4088-3   AACR2

Contents

A People and Their Land

Soaking Up The Hoarfrost

Hoarfrost is frozen fog, the mountain winter's most delicate and destructive moment. A million, shimmering frozen patterns crack tree limbs and snap power lines.

I first discovered hoarfrost the day after Christmas, 1954. The early morning drive to Newfound Gap had been slow and dark through fog and clouds. Suddenly at about 4,500 feet, the sky spread pure blue over a sea of white clouds. Hoarfrost glittered on spruce and white pine where the fog had been. My dad left three of us boys—I was fourteen—at the Gap, 5,048 feet high in the Great Smoky Mountains. We walked all day through two feet of snow in five-degree weather, sixteen miles across Mount LeConte, down by Rainbow Falls to the Cherokee Orchard near Gatlinburg.

The next time I really saw hoarfrost was twenty-three years later, January 26, 1978. It was near dusk, and I was walking along narrow Highway 411 outside Maryville. Wildwood, where I would spend the night at Garland De-Lozier's farm, was not far. Three miles to the north was Porter Middle School, called Porter Academy when Sam Houston attended in 1807–09. To the south were the foothills of the Smokies—the highest mountains in the eastern United States. The Cherokee Indians camped there when a bored, runaway teen-ager, the same Houston, lived with them.

The biting wind kept sneaking through my heavy boots, three pairs of socks, long handles, red-and-black shirt, sweater, jacket, gloves, and cap. How had the Cherokees and Houston survived such cold?

That morning I had stood on the steps of the front porch of the house where I grew up, 121 Ruth Street, Maryville. The trombone player's slide, like the fog, had frozen. (Four University of Tennessee marching band members were walking with me: Alexander's Washboard Band!)

The red-nosed Knoxville television man discovered that his camera motor had frozen, too. (The television crew, along with some uncomfortable newspaper reporters hidden in heated automobiles, were aghast, because I was beginning in this way a campaign for the governorship of Tennessee, which I would win in November.)

The dusk settled. I could see DeLozier's farmhouse. The sparkling hoarfrost still dominated everything. I saw it glisten as I hadn't seen it in twenty-three years because, while walking, I was taking time to look. The wind had whipped an edging of snow in the same place on each telephone pole along the south side of the road—exact and straight, a clean half inch in width. I saw, too, foggy breath from a horse's mouth, funny icicles on cows' tails (when you're walking, cows are everywhere), and fox tracks in the snow. The tracks were not a dog's. There were whisk marks between each one. That comes from the sweep of a fox's tail.

At DeLozier's farm, I got close to the hot fire, ate a big supper, swapped stories with twenty or thirty friends—many new friends—and piled into bed at 9:30. The hound barked at 3:00 A.M. I didn't care.

I had finished the first day of a six-month, 1,022 mile walk across Tennessee. (Does the sound of any other state's name have a finer ring to it?) I would visit with everyone I could find and spend the night with seventy-four different families, most of whom I'd never known before.

When I began my walk that first morning, my father was a little embarrassed. It was, after all, his front porch that was being televised. My mother was concerned for my safety. The hazards turned out to be trucks of all sizes, dogs, and lightning—in that order.

My plan to shake one thousand hands a day wasn't a big, immediate success. One of the first citizens to whom I offered my hand measured me deliberately with his stare and slowly rolled up his truck window.

I had lived in Tennessee for thirty-seven years—my family had lived here for eight generations. I had not yet left the area where I had grown up, but already I had seen the hoarfrost and some other things I hadn't paid attention to for a long time, as well as a couple of things I'd never noticed before.

There was a lot more to see and still more than a thousand miles to go.

I was ready to soak it up . . . hoarfrost, and more.

Stop Trying To Make It Just One Place!

The "Officials" have always insisted that Tennessee ought to stick together. How can it be a real, successful *place* if it doesn't stick together?

Despite the Official huffing and puffing, Tennessee keeps unsticking.

No one should be surprised. Indians, the first Tennesseans, couldn't keep it together. The Chickasaws held the bluffs where Memphis is now. The Creeks and the Crows maintained their separate crossing places on the Tennessee River. Cherokees headquartered at Tanasi, in a remote and fertile mountain river valley.

The state grew unevenly and from different directions. When Tennessee quit being western North Carolina in 1796, Andrew Jackson, David Crockett, and most other Tennesseans lived in the mountainous East. It had only been sixteen winters since James Robertson and John Donelson had walked and canoed from what is today Kingsport to settle Nashville. In 1829, only 663 citizens lived in Memphis when Sam Houston stopped his river trip to send word to Nashville that he would fight anyone who slandered Eliza Allen, the young Gallatin belle who married and then left Houston—plunging him to such despair that he resigned the governorship of Tennessee.

The Officials tried to even things up by inventing the Three Grand Divisions of Tennessee: East, Middle, and West. Historians, politicians, and other tub-thumpers have

harrumphed about the splendor of these geographical divisions nearly as often as Jackson has been enshrined in Tennessee's history.

The concept invaded the state's jurisprudence. The constitution, for example, distributed supreme court justices across the state by Grand Division. Later, signs at every state line welcome center proclaimed: "Welcome to the Three Grand Divisions of Tennessee!"

The War Between the States was, of course, the greatest "unsticker" of all. On the face of it, Tennessee stayed intact. It was the last state out of the Union and the first one back in. The only trouble was: the Grand Division of East Tennessee, by and large, didn't go.

When Tennessee seceded, Scott County, by a unanimous vote of its county court, seceded from Tennessee. The first congressional district of Tennessee, high in the mountains, sent more boys to fight for the Union than any district of the North. Confederate troops occupied Knoxville. Yankees occupied Nashville. Middle and West Tennessee produced Confederate heroes. Parson Brownlow's pro-Union diatribes in the *Knoxville Journal* were the toast of the North.

More of that rivalry is left over than some people will admit. John I. Morgan remembers when there was one, only one, Democrat family on Roan Mountain: The other residents called them Rebels. N. T. Richardson remembers that his *mother* rode a horse from Grand Junction to Chattanooga to warn folks that the Yankees were coming. Some West Tennesseans still can't tell the difference between Republicans and cross-eyed roosters. Whisper Parson Brownlow's name in Franklin, and fine china will rattle.

After the war, it took one hundred years to resurrect the two-party political competition that once starred the disciples of Jackson versus those of Henry Clay, fierce brawls that produced three U.S. presidents. And in 1980, the Democratic nominee for president carried mostly the Confederate areas, and the Republican nominee carried the counties that wouldn't secede.

Federal programs encouraged the divisions. The Appalachian Regional Commission helped East Tennesseans, even though Memphis blacks and rural West Tennesseans were as hard up as any mountaineer.

Things weren't sticking together at all. Some revisionists even began to blame the Grand Divisions. The Officials changed the signs to say: "Welcome to the *Great* State of Tennessee." It was right to change the signs, even though it was done for the wrong reason. A better sign would read: "Welcome to Tennessee, a land of places and people."

It should be plain by now that Tennessee is not just one place. Each of its ninety-five counties, spread across six hundred miles, demands individual attention. A favor for Washington County is no favor for Sullivan County.

And the communities? Give them their independence, too. Try mixing Milan and Humboldt, Manchester and Tullahoma. Each insists on its differences. Brawls over school consolidation can last for years.

The families in the communities? Well, they hold their ground. Chances are good that a Masters is from Unicoi County. There are more than one thousand Naves in Carter County. Huffstetlers and Teffetellers are from Blount; Wood and Woods from Henderson; and Rankins have been in Jefferson for eight generations. And they all can fight. Congressman Rod R. Butler once became so enraged with the Taylor family of Happy Valley that he passed a law changing the name of Taylorsville to Mountain City.

Stick together?

Bristol is closer to Ontario, Canada, than it is to Memphis. Memphis is closer to Houston, Texas, than it is to Mountain City.

Look at the Nolichucky River as it tumbles through the eastern mountains from North Carolina. Compare the Hatchie River as it winds by Bolivar towards the Mississippi. Both rivers are wet and run west. They have little else in common.

Run your fingers through the Mississippi River valley's alluvial soil in Lake County, then through the soil of the Doe

River valley in Johnson County. They are 540 miles apart. Each claims the best soil in America. Both may be right, but nothing else, including most of the crops, is the same.

Listen to Tennessee's music. Nashville is the world's Music City. It has more songwriters, producers, artists, and studios than anywhere else. But Nashville's music and its musicians come from east and west.

Memphis—240 miles west—has been the stirring pot for America's popular music. The Mississippi River and mid-South trade mixed together New Orleans jazz and hill-billy complaining, field chants and hollers, white folks and black folks, rock and roll, rhythm and blues, honky-tonk and pop, W. C. Handy and Furry Lewis, Frankie and Johnny, and Elvis Presley. A musical era exploded from the hot sun and mud of the cotton fields, the river, and Beale Street.

The valleys and coves of the mountains—two hundred miles east of Nashville—protected eight generations of Tennesseans while they handed down a new style of music and unique customs. The Scotch-Irish and English mountaineers collected their instruments from the world: dulcimers from England and Germany, guitars from Spain, and bagpipes from Scotland. They added a fifth string to the African banjo and proclaimed it a new American instrument. But the ancestors of the fifth string—or drone string—must have been the three drone tones of the bagpipe and the drone A string of the first fiddles.

Bluegrass music and country dancing came from these mountains. This is *real* American entertainment. Yet clog dances are offshoots of old Scottish army dances: don't move above the waist and arms straight at the side. The music—especially the sound of fiddles at hoedowns and the break-downs—seems miraculously lifted from Brigadoon. In truth it was. Visit Edinburgh in August for the "Golden Fiddle Awards," an annual concert of the two hundred best Scottish fiddlers. The music could come from the Grand Ole Opry stage; the musicians' faces look like faces in Cocke, Hancock, Carter, or Johnson Counties.

When people can't even agree on how to hunt a red fox,

there is no way to make a state into one stuck-together place.

Compare the hunting habits of the citizens in Belle Meade and Walden's Creek. About the only similarity in their pursuits is that the fox is rarely caught.

Belle Meade, in Middle Tennessee, shares with Palm Beach, Palm Springs, and Bloomfield Hills, Michigan, the distinction of being one of four cities in America with the highest family incomes. There, a special civility reigns.

Walden's Creek, nestled two hundred miles to the east in the foothills of the Smokies, includes families who get along on some of the lowest incomes. There, mountain beauty is king.

On November 1, the hunters and horses from Belle Meade and thereabouts gather in formal ceremony for the blessing of the hounds. Their customs are indistinguishable from those of the fox hunters who trample the meadows and jump the fences each September at Burleigh Castle north of London.

Running behind the fox is the pack of hounds. Next come galloping horses ridden by hunters in formal "pink coats." The entourage plunges through the woods and over the fences each weekend until April 1, when matters are adjourned until the May Steeplechase.

The hunters at Walden's Creek have a little different style. To begin with, like some foxes, these hunters prefer to roam at night. They pick a cool evening in the autumn, climb a ridge, build a bonfire for sitting and talking, and let loose the hounds.

None of these night hunters chases the fox. A horse could never make it through the rough land, especially at night. Not many of these citizens own a horse anyway.

Instead, they listen for the hounds. The hounds are the important thing. Crying and yelping through the hollows, the hounds chase the fox. Each hunter knows the sound of *his* dog. And there is great suspense until the leader of the pack of hounds first is heard.

One famous leader of the pack was "Old Limber," an aged blue tick hound when his seventy-one-year-old master, "Uncle Alf" Taylor, was elected governor of Tennessee in

1920. "Uncle Alf" told voters he was not too old to lead the state if "Old Limber" was not too old to lead the pack. Alf, a good fiddler, also used to say, "There is no finer melody on this green earth than the barking of the dogs echoing through the night as they chase the fox." Roy Acuff's friend and dobro player, "Brother Oswald" Kirby, says fox hunters in his native Walden's Creek often improved the thrill of that heavenly music by enjoying sips of corn likker from Ball jars.

That should prove it. Tennessee is not one place. All of the Official hurrahs for 185 years have not glued it together. It is too long, too narrow, too populated with fiercely independent people in too many different places to stick together. So why try to make it something it is not?

My friend Roy Blount, Jr., says that people should sound like where they grew up, that it's when they start trying to sound like something else that they get messed up. Be what you are. It applies to states, too.

A British travel agent complained to me last summer about "Mud Island," just off the bluffs of Memphis in the Mississippi River. People won't come to such a terrible sounding place, he was sure. Change the name to Paradise Island, or Pirate Island, or something, he said.

He's dead wrong. Mud Island is Mud Island! If the British want to see flame azalea, they can visit Chattanooga in June. If they want to stomp their feet to country music, they can come to Nashville anytime. But, if they want to soak up the hugeness of the mighty Mississippi and the noises of a big, rumbling cotton and trading town with a rowdy history of blues, blacks, whites, cotton, and mud that nothing else in America approaches, well, then they must come to Mud Island and Memphis!

Differences are vanishing everywhere, and sprawls are swallowing places.

But Tennesseans still insist on their differences, even celebrate them . . . and it is a rare Tennessean who doesn't have a place, even if it is a patch, which he prizes.

A Thousand Wonders

There is so much more.

There is a wonderful manner of speaking, if you will listen: The county attorney general's docket is so full that it would "strangle a hog."

There are some strong arguments. "Short-leafed laurel is called rhododendron!" "No, call it laurel!"

There are important customs to remember. If a man gives you a knife, give him a penny in return. It seals the bond of friendship. J. C. Hopkins gave me a knife at lunch one day at his store on Highway 107. Carl Jones in Johnson City taught me the lesson. There are some other knife manners you should know: For instance, you hand a knife back exactly the way it was handed to you.

There are fairs, and high school basketball and football games. Fairs with prizes and carnivals consume August and September. High school football is the attraction on Fridays, September through November. Basketball dominates Tuesday and Thursday nights, January through March. Don't schedule *anything* else. The Mosheim-MacDonald elementary school basketball rivalry in Greene County has all the intensity of the University of Tennessee versus Alabama on Saturday afternoon. And the citizen who risks his life more often than anyone else during these seasons is the game referee, not the local police officer.

Something must be said about the food. Tennessee families love to eat, to share their food, and to talk about it. A guest for supper (dinner is a lunchtime meal in the smaller towns) can expect chicken, roast beef, meat loaf, boiled potatoes, salad, hot biscuits, some more vegetables, two or three desserts, and iced tea. (Iced tea should *always* be served in an extra big glass!) "Have some more. Don't you like the beans?"

Then, for breakfast: country ham, bacon, eggs ("Only two?"), orange juice, grits, hot biscuits and red-eye gravy, honey, some oatmeal if you want it. "Are you sure you've

had plenty?" Such meals are served in modest homes from South Central and Thorn Hill to Niota and Jackson. The only thing more wonderful is a backyard neighborhood or church potluck supper, which you can find on a summer evening in Collinwood or, for that matter, in most any other community in Tennessee.

There are great issues to consider. Should the duck season be split? Should rangers in the Smoky Mountain Park kill the wild boars, or should they be left for the hunters at Tellico? Why can't someone stock Watauga Lake with fish? What about the trap set for a weasel or a mink that catches a dog? What was the dog doing loose? What was the trap doing around the dog? Someone in half of Tennessee's families has a hunting and fishing license.

There are some wise old rules about meeting people: befriend a stranger the way you befriend a dog; let him get to know you; don't try to get to know him.

There are lessons to learn. Study the plain logic of why there are new wood burning stoves in homes everywhere. To get electricity up the hollow to your house, the Tennessee Valley Authority had to build a dam, or a steam plant, or a nuclear power plant, string thick wires high on steel towers hundreds of miles across the state, and put in switches and transformers. You had to pay to put in plugs and central heating. Anyone with a little sense could have figured out it would have been cheaper to cut some wood and burn it in a stove. The stove pays for itself in a year or so with today's high electric rates.

There is a lot to see, besides the hoarfrost, if you will look.

The arrival of spring at a walker's pace is a thousand wonders. There is a warm day in February, but no sign of spring. The long handles stay on! The first week of March comes. People work outdoors, cutting down honeysuckle, cleaning and fixing yards and farms. Still it is chilly. Day-by-day, patches of green grow in the brown fields in Carter's Valley. March 13, bright and sunny, brings two pickup trucks to Cherokee Lake. These first fishermen catch three white bass. A week later, there is movement around the boat docks. Coreopsis, daffodils, forsythia—even dandelions—spread throw rugs of yellow throughout Powell Valley. Rains seem warmer. Creeks run high. Redbuds, then dogwoods, peek from behind tiny new leaves sprouting on the branches of bigger trees. April becomes May. Days are longer and hotter. The pastures of Grassy Cove grow thick.

Is Watt's Bar Lake the only place in the world where a dam, a steam plant, and a nuclear reactor all generate electricity side-by-side? It is an astonishing view.

The rebuilt courthouse at Dayton hosts the opening night of *Inherit the Wind*. It is the story of The Scopes Trial, replayed upstairs in the building exactly where William Jennings Bryan and Clarence Darrow performed for the world in 1925. Reading about it twenty-five years ago started me toward law school.

Rattle 'n Snap and the other magnificent pre-Civil War homes dominate the road between Spring Hill and Mt. Pleasant. There are more fine, old homes at LaGrange. Driving by takes only a few minutes. Walking, you marvel at the architecture.

Then, walk along Beale Street. Close your eyes. Try to recreate the rambunctious past that was once there. So much of it is gone today.

Finally, stick your feet in the Mississippi mud. If you've walked for six months, it's worth doing.

To consider a walk across the state strange is itself strange. That walking should become today's favorite sport says something about what we have come to. It reminds me of the time I asked Johnny Cash why, after twenty-five years at the top of the music business, he still travels and performs more than two hundred nights a year. His look told me that my question was stranger than his schedule. "That's what I do." he said. "What else would I do?" I suppose my father would have said the same thing to anyone who asked why he walked from Maryville to Alnwick to teach school, ten miles round trip each day. That is how he got there. How else would he have gotten there? We didn't have a car until I was nine years old. I suppose most others walked, too. No one asked why.

A great many people remember candidates for public office who walked into their yards, spent some time on their front porches, had supper, and even stayed the night. It was a logical way to do things. It still is.

If I had kept a journal during my walk, or if I had a little more time now, I might tell the rest of these stories. But I didn't keep a journal. I was too tired each night to write much down. More importantly, I wanted to *experience* the walk, not write about it. I wanted to soak it all up—the places and the people.

Now I want to share my experience, the wonder of the places and people of Tennessee.

To do that, I recruited Robin Hood, a Pulitzer Prize winning photographer from Chattanooga. He and his friend, Barry Parker, toured the state—twenty-five thousand miles in six months—capturing Tennessee on film and on paper.

To put things together, I asked Sam Moore at Thomas Nelson Publishers in Nashville to help. He and his staff have assembled Robin's stunning photography and Barry's sensitive writing into this magnificent book: *The Tennesseans: A People and Their Land*.

Let me warn you: This book is not about *all* of Tennessee. It is a walk across the state, giving you only a taste of Tennessee. If you are a Tennessean, you're bound to enjoy this taste. If you're not, after learning what our state is like, you'll probably wish you lived here.

You're welcome to join us, to help soak up the hoarfrost and number our wonders . . . *if* you'll be careful not to mess things up. There is one thing more: You must promise to help us celebrate and preserve our differences and never to join the Officials who try to make us just one place.

LAMAR ALEXANDER
July, 1981

The Tennesseans

A PEOPLE AND THEIR LAND

Maryville

    Ninety-three-year-old Heddie Willocks rakes red maple leaves outside her Maryville home. Her mottled hands draw the rake in strong, brisk sweeps. She was born on the farm, built fences, and drove horse teams—and knows, she says, the blessing of hard work. Every few minutes now she must rest, leaning her bonneted head against the tree. Even Heddie must bow to age. Shortly, she has her wind back and renews her attack on the lawn. She stiff-walks to a stray leaf floating gently to the ground and draws it into her pile.

3

Blount County settlers were small farmers, not wealthy planters. The rugged Scotch-Irish and others breached the mountains into Tennessee, hungering for freedom and cheap, fertile land, and found both. They claimed the rich, rolling earth around Maryville, built their forts and grist mills on a grid of streams and rivers, then settled into the cupped and sheltered coves. They brought their families, their belongings, and the emotional tools needed to tame a mountainous land—an aggressive belief in hard work, frugality, self-reliance, and the fear of God.

There were always chores in an endless cycle of planting, tending, gathering, and mending. Children carried water buckets to workers in the field, and the presentation of a first hoe to a child was a time for celebration—a rite of passage into the hardscrabble life.

"What counts in this life
is a place to spend eternity."
—Heddie Willocks, Maryville

Dusk, Great Smoky Mountains

Hester "Heddie" Willocks

Wade Caylor

5

Maynard Headrick, Miller's Cove

The frontier allowed for the nonconformist and the rugged individualist. And they still exist. Millard Fillmore Carroll lives with his honeybees and blue tick hounds in the woods flanking Chilhowee Mountain. At night, he sits in lantern light at the steps of his shack and strokes his dogs. He cusses city ways, and his cackle pierces the dark woods. The old trapper would rather listen to the creek "just a ticklin'" by his door and the yelp of his dogs than to the clamor in the valley. Living up here alone, says Millard, means freedom and peace. "C'mon boys," he yells to his wriggling band of hounds as he turns back up a dirt road to his woods.

6

Cable homeplace, Cades Cove

Settlers handed down a wry humor to combat a hard life. In a general store, two farmers play checkers with bottle caps and swap stories that begin "Times were so bad" and end with "We fought over lumps in the gravy cause we thought it was meat," or "We cried trying to reach the white crock doorknobs 'cause we thought they were biscuits." Their talk is peppered with exaggerated images from farm life: So-and-so has enough money to burn he could dry a wet dog or is so tight he wouldn't give a dime to see a doodlebug eat a bale of hay.

Cades Cove

"I'm seventy-two and done it all—logged, cut timber, made whiskey, and done a little of everything in the world there was to do. I accepted the Lord in nineteen hundred and fifty-six. Never did make another drop."
—Tomie Sellers with hubcaps in Wear's Cove near Maryville

8

Millard Fillmore Carroll, Chilhowee Mountain

Little River

Headrick's Chapel, Wear Valley

"Without Maryville College, an awful lot of us would have never gotten a college education. It was our stepping stone."

—Dr. A. Randolph Shields, author, reared in Cades Cove

Bart Suttles and Leona Mae, Wildwood Grocery

Their music, like their talk, filled a deep need. Boys picked up guitars, fiddles, banjos, dobros, and dulcimers and taught themselves to play—and play well. At huskings, a jug of home brew was placed in the middle of a pile of corn, and the first one to shuck his way to the jug got the first drink. Afterward, they fiddled and buckdanced all night.

Bart Suttles said he was too sickly to sing, but there he was in the corner of the store in front of the rainbow-colored detergent boxes with his thumbs hooked inside his suspenders and a worn, static-sputtering electric guitar dangling across his stomach. As a farm boy, he had won a guitar by selling seed, listened to Maybelle Carter through the crackle of the old radio, and taught himself to play in the quiet mountain evenings. For years the guitar had been silent, but now he sang the old whimsical ballads, verse after verse. His eyes sparkled, he rolled his bony shoulders, his mustache spread across his face. His wife blushed. His voice rose from a soft drawl to a yodel to a mule skinner's yelp. The guitar sputtered, but Bart just sang louder, singing his way back to the huskings of his youth.

The old man fingered the hewed logs at the Oliver Cabin in Cades Cove. It all came back vividly, he said: Chicken feed dropped through slats in the floor, snow piling up in the corner on a winter's night. He grew up in such a cabin. Now he is confounded by his grandson who wants to return to the rustic life. The boy and his wife are building a cabin. Just as the old man fled from the hardships of pioneer life, the young couple are eagerly embracing it, fleeing from something else. The old man smiled. It's come full circle, hasn't it.

12

French mill, Dumplin Creek

Boyd's Creek—Dumplin Valley

Randle is always up early, feeding heifers over fence posts sugared with frost. He moves through the mist, his breath whistling through his teeth, to his son's house across the road where he raps on the back door each morning and yells, "You up?" While the family eats breakfast, he fidgets in the den, joking how the others "just goof around." At seventy-one, he is still square in the shoulders and thick in the chest. He yells because he is hard of hearing and fusses because that's his way.

He is retired, but no one works harder. He is anxious to get going, to top off the bin with soybeans while the earth is dry. All day long he pulls the grain wagon back and forth to the barn, sending the beans up the noisy auger. Only when the bin is full and the earth begins to purple and cool does he climb from the tractor and lie in the threshings to daydream.

15

Henry's Crossroads Methodist Church, Kodak

Long before tractors, Randle planted with mules, pitched hay with a team, picked corn by hand. Up at 4:00 A.M. with a coal oil lantern, he chopped wood for the stove, broke the ice skim in the pail. Life has been a litany of hard work, a song of sweat, a pride in tasks done well. He boasts he never drew a check from a public job and is saddened that so many have left the family farms. (His grandson, Randy [Randle III], will make the fifth generation of Kykers to farm at Alder Branch.) He is the rural traditionalist who believes you work what you've got, help your neighbors when you can, and avoid owing others. "I like to see where I'm agoin'," he shouts, easing the tractor around a curve—an apt summation of his life.

16

Arthur Berrier, Mutton Hollow

Sunset at Alder Branch

"The first settlers dug out these ditches, cleared these fields so that I could have it now. We have to appreciate what these people have done for us. I'm old enough to get sentimental about it."
—James Hardin, neighbor of the Kykers at Alder Branch

The son is made of the father and is, therefore, partly of the land. But his gaze goes beyond. Inside the glass cage of the combine, the soybean dust boiling up around the sides, R. A. (Randle Jr.) talks more of tax breaks, borrowing power, and cash flow than of crops. His mind wanders afield of the beans he's picking and the new roof he needs on the tractor shed. One foot is squarely in farming, but the other rests squarely with a host of business schemes. R. A. may harvest crops in the morning, then at lunch scan computer printouts of a growing sales force he heads. He may mend fences in the afternoon, check on a subdivision project in the evening, and direct a sales meeting at night. Even when he carries tobacco to auction at Newport, he banters about his outside interests.

Still the ties that bind R. A. to the land are strong. It's fun to work your own spread, he says, and be your own boss. Farming is the last outpost of the free enterpriser. "I'll never leave my home base here," he vows. So the father and son differ and fuss loud enough to be heard down the cedar-lined road and sometimes grouse with each other in the field. And R. A. reads his printout at the kitchen table while his father waits impatiently in the den.

Soybean harvest, Alder Branch

19

Rakes at Cook Mill

Joe Hicks, Boyd's Creek

"*A farm is not a place to grow wealthy; it is a place to grow corn.*"
—Andrew Lytle, *I'll Take My Stand*

Hayrake, Dumplin Creek

Jonesboro

On a late afternoon, the Chester Inn in Jonesboro is a peaceful landmark, fronted by a rambling white porch with graceful brackets and balusters. But in 1803, there were sounds of angry men on Main Street. Followers of John Sevier, first governor of Tennessee, talked of tarring and feathering their rival, the popular and fiery Judge Andrew Jackson, who lay sick with flu inside the inn. With the boldness that stamped his life, Jackson set a loaded pistol on either bedstand, informed the crowd that he awaited their arrival, and asked that the leader of the mob kindly be first in line. The invitation was declined, and the crowd dispersed.

23

"He was the noblest work of God. An honest man."
—Inscription on tombstone of David Deaderick, October 10, 1754—October 20, 1823, Jonesboro cemetery

The buildings of old Jonesboro beg to be listened to. Up and down the lantern-lined streets of the state's oldest town, buildings talk of rough and tumble frontier days when disputes were settled with dueling pistols or fists, of a town cleaved by the war, of the great dusty stage road to the West and the coming of the trains. It's two centuries of history written in bricks and mortar and planks.

At the corner of First and Main, a leaf-covered yard is all that's left where the busy print shop once stood. The two-story building is gone, but the aura of Elihu Embree lingers. Once a slave owner, Embree became a zealot for the abolitionist cause. Here in 1819 and 1820, he published the first two periodicals in the nation devoted exclusively to denouncing slavery.

25

Jonesboro Presbyterian Church

"*I'd say there are ghosts in this town. If you know your history, you feel the presence of those who have lived here. We refer to the idiosyncracies of people long dead and gone in a very loving way.*"
—Dorothy Wood, Jonesboro

Grave of Katharine Emmerson, first mayor of Knoxville, old Jonesboro cemetery

Down the street the fluted columns and louvered shutters in the belfry add to the classical symmetry and sense of proportion of the Presbyterian Church. But something is out of kilter. There is rancor inside, the murmur of a congregation divided over their wartime loyalties. Northern partisans leave and build a church two blocks away.

Then there are the Masons and Dillworths. The Masons' sympathies lay with the North; the Dillworths' with the South. They lived on either end of a partitioned home in Jonesboro. When Northern troops marched into town, the Dillworths pushed their valuables through a hole in the attic for safekeeping with the Masons, and vice versa when Rebel forces arrived. The families stayed friends and allies throughout the war. No partition could block their concern for each other.

Sadness cloaked the handsome brick home with the stepped gable roof on the south side of Main. Inside, a family mourned the loss of their son. Captain Zed T. Willett left West Point in his senior year, said good-bye to his family, joined the 19th Tennessee Infantry, and died early in the war, April 7, 1862, at Shiloh.

Old Sweetshop Ice Cream Parlor

Historical Jonesboro Days

Forgotten gate

The Mansion House was one of the fashionable inns that lined Main Street when it was the Great Stage Road from Abingdon, Virginia, to the West. The rumble of the stagecoach and the shouts of the driver signaled another arrival. One passenger climbed down from the high seat beside the driver. Five more weary travelers stumbled from the coach with the inelegance of a people settling a country.

A house faces the ditch that Little Limestone Creek cuts through town. A porch swing moves slightly in the breeze as if someone just got up, but there is no one here, just the creek in front and, to Dr. S. B. Cunningham's eternal chagrin, the tracks in back. Doctor Cunningham gave up surgery to build a railroad. His passion was to watch the East Tennessee and Virginia roll by from his porch swing, but when they named him railroad president and laid the line, the grade forced the tracks to run behind his home and not in front.

First frost

Washington County Courthouse

Washington County Courthouse boasts imposing Corinthian columns that are repeated in smaller form in the cupola. The building is monumental against the scale of the two-story town, but then Jonesboro's significance to the state has been out of all proportion to its size—the capital of the State of Franklin, the seat of the state's oldest county. Future giants of state and national government strolled the streets. In 1788, David Allison, John McNairy, Joseph Hamilton, Archibald Roane, and Andrew Jackson were admitted to the bar at Jonesboro's first courthouse. Among them, they served in three judgeships, as governors of two states, in both houses of Congress, as major general, as the hero of the War of 1812, and as president of the United States.

31

Ray Martin, Shady Valley

The Mountains

The eastern boundary of Tennessee is formed by the great tree-covered Unaka Mountains, which include the highest peaks east of the Rockies. The Unakas are among the most lush and ruggedly beautiful mountains of the Appalachian chain. Once as craggy as the Himalayas, these Tennessee mountaintops have been worn and rounded by ages of wind and rain. Where the Unakas widen at Gatlinburg, they are called the Great Smoky Mountains. These old mountains are not so much awesome as inspirational, less an adventure than a retreat.

33

Appalachian Trail at Grassy Bald

A farmer living on the slope of the mountain reaches out to shake hands, his fingers brown and gummy from grading tobacco, a sign of fall as certain as the changing leaves. Another farmer twirls a shucked ear of corn into the air, letting it fall to the music of his granddaughter's laughter. Soon the crib will be full. A farm boy stands beside the road, breathless and shaken from killing his first hog. "We thought it was done dead and laid it on the table and it was still kicking," he says, recoiling from the vision. "Whooee," he says, shaking his head, "I didn't like the part about sticking it none."

In the mountains, beauty springs from utility. So too does the beauty of Delia Troutman. She is a small, lively woman, her thick gray hair pulled back in a bun, her smiling face craned upward, her hands clapping with glee at her own jokes. Her quick, darting movements, her constant busyness, long ago earned her the nickname, Cricket. Cricket is eighty ("Oops, now I've gone and told my age!")—a child of the mountains. She has always lived beneath the shadow of Roan Mountain and the high balds, and here she will stay. "Come on anytime you'uns want to," she says at parting. "If we're living, you'll find us at home."

34

Glen Taylor, Dry Creek

Zionville Baptist Church, on North Carolina state line at Trade

Carter County school bus

Chimney smoke curls from hills that dome up like a thick pea soup at boil, hills so steep that cattle graze cross-legged and farmers use horse-drawn mowers instead of tractors—not out of poverty but by necessity. Their farms are stitched along the creeks that tumble down the hollows. Moored to the road by a bucking footbridge, the houses and outbuildings ride the swells and sinks of the land.

Bernice Hatley attacks the mad geometry of the mountains. She roars up the rocky, single-lane roads in her bright Carter County school bus, a garish swirl of yellow and blinking red against the pablum gray of November. Up Sugar Hollow and Green Hollow and Dye Leaf Road she goes, downshifting through hairpin turns, rushing past the sloping fields where hens flap around the cattle, roaring past clotheslines strung like banners and shiny hubcaps on barn walls and rusting junkers in the creeks, climbing deep into the hollows where few ever go. The bus stops at a board and batten house, Bernice opens the door and out pop two tow-headed boys and a freckle-faced girl with a sweater tied about her waist, all bounding from the door, satchels flying, met by their mother and three mongrels whose tails whip the air in fierce delight. Bernice has time for a "howdy," little else, then roars away up the mountain road.

Sugar Hollow

"*My mountains . . . their scale is not awe inspiring, but human; their charm not striking, but subtle. Yet these mountains possess a classic elegance, a regularity of form, a graceful symmetry in the rounded heights, covered in green to their summits.*"

—Jerome Doolittle, *The Southern Appalachians*

Denver Crum, Cedar Creek

Shaw Farthing farm, Highway 159 at North Carolina state line

Roan Mountain at North Carolina state line

A high-arching bridge spans the dark green water of Lake Watauga. The reservoir looks stamped with a cookie cutter from the mountains that enfold it. A gale blows down the lake, kicking up whitecaps and tugging at a man walking the bridge. On the long climb up Roan Mountain at midnight, a car is ambushed by leaves whipped up from the roadbed by a coiling wind. At the summit, a van shudders in the eerie blow. Subtract three degrees each thousand feet you climb and add a new dimension to the words *wind* and *cold* when you're in the mountains.

Roan's Creek

40

Randy Garland and "Cadillac," Doe River Valley

"Got your apples. Down by the river, your black-berries." Shaw Farthing is pointing to the mammoth nooks and crannies on his mountain farm. "Every holler's got a spring in it. Best water in the country. Plenty of good air in the wintertime. God, it's rich land," he says, beaming. "Yes, sir, everything you need." Will he ever sell the land? No, sir. It goes to the children. As for Shaw, they'll bury him (he again points) in the family plot on that high ridge—no better place to ride the great, green swells forever.

Trade, eastern-most community in Tennessee

Lewis Chandler, Allen Gap

41

Powell Valley

In this beautiful countryside, time has bent back upon itself. Not long ago, life here was primitive. A man was his own cooper and cobbler, his own doctor and wheelwright. As a boy, Marcellus Moss Rice went to neighbors in Union County to borrow embers for a fire. His son-in-law, Glen Irwin, remembers TVA coming to the valley in the thirties to build the first of the great dams just up the road at Norris. One farmer grieved over the loss of his rich bottomland to the waters. He took a gun and killed himself. But the power poles went up, and the lights went on.

43

TVA, a corporation "clothed with the power of government, but possessed of the flexibility and initiative of a private enterprise," built a staircase of dams that kept the rampaging Tennessee River in check and turned the flow of water to power. There were other major benefits from TVA: flood control, beautiful lakes for recreation, the increase in barge traffic, and the production of fertilizer. It took an area where poor land practices were depleting the soil and turned it green again. But soon water power alone was not enough to fill the need for electricity, and the giant utility built steam-powered plants that fed on huge quantities of coal. The men in Powell Valley keep mining the coal, bringing it out of deep shafts in the mountains and scooping it from open pits. Dwight Lindsay moves back in time, belly-down on the belt that winds into Cross Mountain. He crawls past coal seams laid down ages ago. He spends his days in a two-foot space shored up with timbers, bolts, and metal plates. Like many men in the valley, he followed his father into the mines to join the fraternity of shared danger.

Carl Bean's pearl inlaid guitar

Come listen you fellows so young and so fine
And seek not your fortune in the dark dreary mine
It will form as a habit and seep in your soul
Till the stream of your blood is black as the coal.

There's many a man that I've known in my day
That lived just to labor his young life away
Like a fiend with his dope and a drunkard his wine
A man will have lust for the lure of the mine.

I hope when I'm gone and the ages shall roll
My body will blacken and turn into coal
Then I'll look from the door of my heavenly home
And pity the miner a-digging my bones.

—Merle Travis, "Dark As a Dungeon"

Levi Collins, Caryville

Dwight Lindsay, Cross Mountain mine

Levi Collins

Coalminer's children, Briceville

One morning, as Glen Irwin and his brother were sowing winter wheat, three men came down the road in a terrible hurry, running back and forth surveying farmland. "Better put up the team in the barn," Glen wisely told his brother. "They're going to be doing something here." The next week at a mass meeting in a schoolhouse, county agents told the farmers to bring in their crops, bale their hay, and prepare to leave their land forever.

The overnight creation of the city of Oak Ridge was an upheaval in the lives of rural East Tennesseans. The site chosen in Anderson County was isolated, yet close to Knoxville and accessible to cheap, plentiful TVA power. In September, 1942, the government purchased 58,880 acres of farmland at forty-five dollars an acre, moved farmers out, and hired thousands of workers to build a city. One prefab house was built every thirty minutes. The project was shrouded in mystery, and the plants where scientists and engineers labored were arbitrarily designated X-10, K-25, and Y-12. Behind the walls, scientists diffused gases of different weights to produce enriched uranium 235, the fissionable fuel at the heart of the atomic bomb. By mid-1945, Oak Ridge, once sleepy farmland, was a community of 82,000 that appeared on no map of the state. About the time Marcellus Moss Rice died just down the road, the atomic age was born.

Nancy Rose, Norris

48

Home of John Rice Irwin

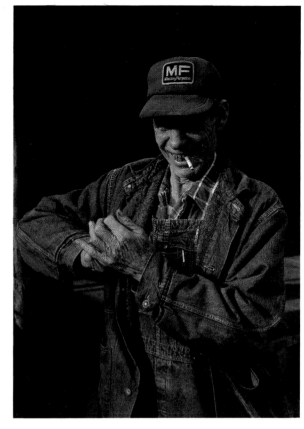

Russell Rose, Norris

Clinch River

Chris Keim, a physicist from the Mellon Institute in Pittsburgh, became part of the army of workers at this secret city in 1944. His job was to help separate the isotope U-235. He was never told the ultimate purpose of the project, but he did know that in separating the isotope there was potential for release of a tremendous amount of energy. Like other scientists at Oak Ridge, he pursued his task while asking few questions. When the bomb was dropped on Hiroshima, his first reaction was disbelief that the whole world should learn the secret the same time as he.

The war ended, but a new frontier had opened; Chris Keim and other scientists stayed on at Oak Ridge. He separated isotopes of other elements: lithium and calcium and copper and nickel and silver and tin. Oak Ridge flourished; the land went public, with churches getting the first pick of lots; the city appeared on the map of the state. Chris Keim is retired now and proud of his adopted city—this enclave of science and culture—and excited by the "unlimited possibilities" in the experiments underway.

Time teases you in Powell Valley. There's a Museum of Appalachia, filled with Stone Age items, and just down the road is the Museum of Atomic Energy. Levi Collins lives in the valley and has brewed whiskey and dug coal. In the 1920s, moonshine making was so open in Tennessee that stills sat on the side of the road and no one bothered you. Then Prohibition passed, and the law came in. "I got scared like a rabbit with hounds after it," says Levi. Later, he went into the mines. These were dust-filled, rat-infested mule mines. But there was a blessing to having the rats. Before a cave-in, they would scurry off, giving a man half a chance to get out before he got buried. In later years, the machines ran the rats off. The early warning system disappeared. So much for progress.

51

Cutting white oak strips for baskets

Big Orange Country

John Ward, radio voice for the University of Tennessee football team, wears his good-luck towel draped like a prayer shawl around his neck. Lean and intense, he hunches over the broadcast table in the glassed-in radio booth seven stories above the field at Neyland Stadium. His clipboard, half-sucked throat lozenge, and cup of ice water are lined up like soldiers in front of him. The play unrolls, and he ministers to a million or more listeners across the state:

"A low end-over-end, driving kick will be taken on the skip by James, to the fifteen, gets outside," (the voice gains a notch in intensity), "gets running room, James to the twenty . . ."

53

The faithful. They have come from all directions on this bright, crisp autumn Saturday, flooding the interstates, floating in boats and yachts up the Tennessee River. Most bear orange, their shibboleth: orange cushions and leg warmers, sweaters and cowboy hats, windbreakers and sunglasses, caps and pom-poms, streamers and tam-o'-shanters. And those fans too far away to make the trip hang near their radios at cookouts, at bars, and at home, listening to Ward's voice:

". . . James to the twenty-five, to the thirty, to the thirty-five, forty, has running room, James to the forty-five, fifty . . ."

Knox County Courthouse and United American Bank building

James White Fort, first settlement in Knoxville

The Fort Sanders section of Knoxville is eerily quiet. Cars are parked bumper-to-bumper along the steep streets of this turn-of-the-century neighborhood flanking the UT campus, but not a soul is in sight. Everyone is at the game, and for a moment, the old homes, now partitioned into student apartments, retreat to an earlier age when Fort Sanders was the tree-lined domain of wealthy industrialists and middle-class merchants. Author James Agee wrote lyrically of Knoxville as it was in the summer of 1915, when fathers on Highland Avenue watered their small lawns in the cool of the evening and the sounds that filled the neighborhood were the chorus of crickets and sweet hiss of the hose. For Agee, it was the innocent age of youth. But the reverie is broken. Another sound is building in swells in the battleship-gray bowl, and it rolls slowly from the stadium to crash against Fort Sanders half a mile away.

". . . To the forty-five, spins off a tackle to the forty," (Ward stays pinned to his chair in the swirl of excitement), "runs through another tackle to the thirty-five . . ."

Rev. Carolyn Harwell, Faith Home Mission, Gay Street

The Nutcracker Ballet, *Knoxville Civic Center Auditorium*

Confluence of the French Broad and Holston Rivers

Knoxville grew as a marketing center for the mountain people. As such, it reflected their conservative spirit. But there was another side to the city, a flamboyance that revealed itself in the Appalachian Conservation Exposition of 1911—an opportunity for the city to advertise itself to the world. The selection of Knoxville as headquarters for TVA, and the growth of the UT campus added facets to the city. Knoxville transformed its Mountain View area into a modernistic development, and once again the city is advertising itself to the world with its international Energy Exposition.

57

Knoxville has always been a city of sharp contrasts: The quiet of a neighborhood against the roar of a game; dour factories and jutting glass buildings; the conservatism of the mountaineer and the gambling instincts of the entrepreneur.

Tchaikovsky's *Nutcracker* breaks across Knoxville Civic Center auditorium. Young ballerinas in clown face prance off stage to explode in a mad scramble of costume changes. Other members of the Maryville-Alcoa Civic Ballet await their cues in the curtained wings. The toy soldier swings his powerful legs. Two teen-age ballerinas exchange whispered encouragement before leaping on stage.

Five minutes before curtain, Maryville-Alcoa Civic Ballet

The Dewdrop Fairy, Yvette Herzbrun, finishes a dance and moves backstage, her tiara sparkling, her eyes brimming with tears. She is limping, her right heel is bleeding, and she wilts in a metal chair. Yvette's cue arrives, and forcing a smile, she soars back on stage. Now the music builds and she runs toward her partner, throwing herself into arms that press her aloft, her own arms spread and locked in perfect execution. Her friends cheer silently backstage, and a triumphant smile replaces the Spartan one as Tchaikovsky's music swells.

The Nutcracker Ballet

"... to the thirty, twenty-five, twenty," (the roar of eighty-five thousand on their feet at Neyland Stadium is joined by a million whoops and cheers across the state) "fifteen, ten, five," (say it, John), "GIVE HIM SIX. TOUCH-DOWN TENNESSEE. Roland James eighty-eight yards on a sterling punt return. And James has given Tennessee the lead."

Saturday at Neyland Stadium

60

Sunset over Neyland Stadium

Grassy Cove

The cove is a few thousand acres of rich grazing land sunk into a crescent-shaped bowl on the Cumberland Plateau. It is crossed by a road that dips down, runs a flat, straight mile by two general stores owned by first cousins, then climbs away. The cove has the pace of men living close to the earth. It is sun-soaked hogs sleeping against the corn shocks and the smell of caked mud on work boots and the slow talk of men sitting out the rain.

63

"My daddy would trade for anything: furs, beeswax, loose sage, ginseng, chickens and eggs, turkeys, chestnuts, dried field peas, squirrels. 'Buy anything—sell everything,' that was his slogan."

—John Kemmer, store owner and rancher, Grassy Cove

It is Bob Hayes, tough and grizzled, who wears an Australian bush hat and smokes a corncob pipe and observes: "Fox hunting—deer hunting. There ain't a damn thing I haven't done. There ain't a damn stump or hollow around this area I don't know about." He clasps a knee in two rough hands. "Country's a hard life, but damn if I don't think it's better for you. Good air. Lay down in the creek and drink like a mule. Used to kill your meat out of the woods—wild hogs, turkey once in a while, mess of squirrel. You walked from here to Crossville. It made a man of you."

Hank Kemmer's home

*"I know I hadn't done anybody any good. But
I hadn't done anybody any bad either."*

—Bob Hayes, ranch foreman, Grassy Cove

The cove is families like the Kemmers with long-standing ties to the land. John Kemmer III, rancher and store owner, is lean of body, movement, and speech. Cousin George, who runs the smaller of the two general stores, is a big, garrulous, ham hock of a man. Gone from John's store are the wood burning stove and patent medicines and heated political discussions and barter-for-anything style of his father's day. But crammed on bulging counters and shelves are watches and wrenches, lightbulbs and lanterns, gumdrops and galluses, horse collars and hiking boots. "General store?" says John. "More like general confusion."

The cove is a dusty-faced cattle and hog rancher known as Grace Brady. She could be mistaken for a male farmhand in her muddy galoshes and ragged corduroy jacket, her thickly braided hair piled under her cap. Working by herself, Grace feeds the cattle before daybreak and stays up nights when the sows have litters. "She's a good old mountain woman," Bob Hayes says of her. "There ain't no foolishness to Grace Brady."

66

Cumberland Plateau

Tom, with pink cheeks and black hair curling out under his cap, and Perry, the self-proclaimed hillbilly, pushed their way through the cold ravine, through the briars and bare limbs and up the slope following Tippi's yapping bark. When they reached the dog, they slowly circled a tall poplar, craning for a glimpse of the squirrel. Perry shook a nearby sapling that set up a clatter. A tail twitched in a high crook of the poplar, and Perry saw it, raised his Browning automatic and fired. The gray squirrel shivered in the hail of shot and hugged his perch. Perry waited. The squirrel tumbled limp and broken to the ground. Tom spotted another in the same tree and quickly shot it.

By now, Curly had arrived. He scooped up the glassy-eyed squirrels and gutted them. "Nice and tender," he chortled. "These young'uns will make mighty fine frying." He stuffed the squirrels in his pouch and wiped the blood caking his hands.

Sequatchie Valley

This is more than blood sport on the plateau. In sport there is waste—wasted shells, wasted meat, wasted movement. Here men hunt woods they can track in their sleep, and the game they shoot will be on the table. For their fathers and grandfathers, eating meant hunting; and since shells were costly, if you could spear or club an animal to death, so much the better. And when the squirrel was killed, the liver was kept, the skull was cracked open and the brains were eaten, the hide was used as wing leather to mend harnesses and shoes. "It was might near self-existence on these mountains," Johnson Swafford, an old-timer, recalls. "People would makeshift whatever they could to get by." This then is the heritage: Everything is used; nothing to waste.

*"I don't work with any pattern.
If it comes out right, it gets made."*
—Nell Fann on quilting

Oren Wooden Orchard, New Harmony

Hermitage Springs

Tom Morgan, Morgan Springs

Johnson Swafford went into the virgin forests that covered the plateau at the turn of the century to cut timber for crossties and barrel staves. Land was so cheap and plentiful his grandfather traded one thousand acres of timber for a wood burning stove. There was no such thing as "select cut," so the land was denuded. Virgin stands of hemlock, pine, oak, and poplar so open a person could drive a wagon through them were replaced by second growth with its understory of saplings, bushes, and brambles. "If they'd had better practices," says Johnson wistfully, "these mountains would have been the garden spot of the world." Still, there is beauty on the plateau; on this broad tabletop of land, the air seems brighter, the sky bigger than in the valley below.

72

Patrick Walsh and Trouble, Donoho Hotel, Red Boiling Springs

Two stout women peel to their T-shirts and poke their ladders into the apple trees at Wooden's Orchard. They are migrants from Florida, up for the fall picking season. The women work furiously, filling canvas waist sacks with apples, pulling the drawstring to dump the apples, racing the sun for eight dollars a bin. Their pace never slackens. They work each tree from bottom up, circling it, bending back branches, picking it clean like bees working a clover patch. At the packing shed, the apples are danced over brush rollers, graded, chilled, and shipped.

In a lower field, men stripped to the waist are heaving pumpkins like medicine balls. These pumpkins are grown as ornaments, not food. A field hand ponders the meaning of it all. "People just buy these pumpkins to cut out the eyes and put a light in them," he says, shaking his head in disbelief. "Ain't that silly?"

"What I like about Tennessee, you can drop a seed and it will come up."

—Texas natives Leo and Nettie Cope, picking apples on Walden's Ridge

Mary Morgan, playing the autoharp

Curly learned to play the fiddle by listening to others. He can't read a note ("looks like flyspecks to me"), but he won a national fiddling championship. He is the consummate performer whose rendition of Johnson's "Old Gray Mule," where he mixes braying with fiddling, has tickled audiences from the *Grand Ole Opry* to the king and queen of Greece. Playing bluegrass with Perry, Tom, and a banjo picker named Ed, Curly winks, makes faces, grimaces, and puckers, his blue-gray eyes on you, playing to you, pushing the music at you, using body English and a bow. "When I play, I play with every fiber of my body," says Curly. Nothing goes to waste.

"You had no entertainment back then except what you made. Buckwing dancing, the double shuffle, that was the prettiest sound you ever heard out of your feet."

—Johnson Swafford, longtime Walden's Ridge resident

Curly Fox

Red Boiling Springs

Rutherford County Courthouse

Johnny Reb monument, courthouse square

Murfreesboro

After Jesse Cobb rattles off how Murfreesboro has the best cafes in Middle Tennessee and the best schools and did you know Uncle Dave Macon, the first *Grand Ole Opry* star, hailed from Rutherford County and how Murfreesboro is at the very geographical center of the state, that's right, and how it once was the state capital and how it is known as a church town, and after he adds another curled cedar shaving or two to the courthouse lawn, he cocks his head and says with a wink, "Now boys, don't think we're not a little prejudiced. We are. It's home."

Brown's Mill, Lascassas

Courthouse square

Windrow's Rockvale Grocery

If you grew up in any middle-sized town in the state, any place small enough for a farmer in overalls to feel comfortable hunkering in the hallway of the courthouse, it's easy to think of Murfreesboro as home. Here sits the typical Tennessee courthouse—cranberry red with white columns and a white cupola that bulges bug-eyed with four clocks that face in four directions. An endless stream of cars and pickups slowly circle the square to organ music from outdoor speakers, and whittlers yak for hours beneath the shade trees on the courthouse lawn. The town's Main Street is lined with large, old trees that turn scarlet in fall and with rambling brick and frame and stucco homes that have trellises in the yard and flags flying from the porch. The town has a Civil War battlefield and the graceful campus of Middle Tennessee State University. It has a re-created log cabin community as a nod to its past, and new bank buildings near the square as testament to its future.

81

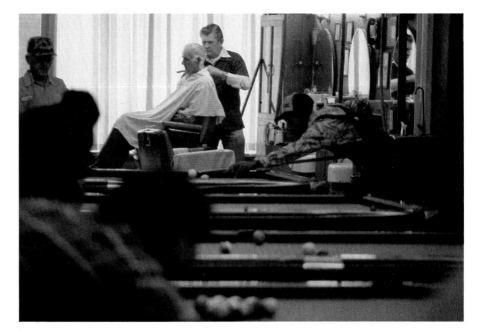

Past Time Pool Hall and Barber

At the Tip Top Barber Shop on the south side of the square, owner Eurel Sauls stops snipping Silly-Putty from a youngster's hair long enough to sell a carton of eggs to an elderly woman. Eurel wears a starched white shirt, a tie, and black wing-tip shoes. He has the polite but crisp way of a country doctor. A friend comes in to talk about a mutual acquaintance who died. The friend sits in an empty barber chair, his eyes glazed, and drones on as Eurel nods and clips.

R. H. "Dick" Stickney shuffles out of the stockroom of his drugstore. At ninety-one, he is the oldest merchant on the square. "I'll stop coming in the day Bubba Woodfin takes me out the front door," he says. At Past Time Pool Hall, a black farmer sinks the eight ball, and a white farmer he is beating raps on the floor with his cue stick for the rack boy.

83

Khadija Jamal, health food restaurant waitress

Sarah is ready with cups and saucers when the City Cafe Coffee Club strolls in at 10:00 A.M. to take their seats at the long table in the back. The newspaper publisher and the preacher, the banker and the lawyer, the jeweler and the undertaker—and a dozen others of assorted professions—meet each morning to drink coffee and decide by a spirited game of numbers who picks up the tab. There are warm-up rounds before the big game, which is followed by a post game. No business or politics is discussed, just a constant chatter that rivals any sewing bee.

Checkers is so popular that they play in the courtroom in the evenings—games of long pauses punctuated by sudden bursts of moves. Across from the courthouse is a vegetarian restaurant with oil paintings of nudes on the walls and, serving the meals, a black girl wearing a flowing caftan and a locket with a scripture from the Koran. And it all fits in smoothly on the square, thank you.

The whittlers sit on the benches and talk knives. "What would you give me for that one?" asks one whittler. "Ever see it with brass up there? Never been sharpened." He picks up shavings and starts clipping them with a pair of snippers. After a pause: "It's a Bullett. That's the name of it, and it was made in Pakistan." Another arrival pulls out his cedar stick from underneath his arm and starts whittling. The policeman on the square claims to have watched the whittlers reduce a truckload of fence posts to shavings.

So it goes in a friendly, relaxed, syncopated way. The clock in the cupola gongs. The cars slowly circle the square. R. H. Stickney shuffles out of the stockroom. Eurel Sauls rings up a three-dollar haircut. The men in the pool hall rap on the floor for the rack boy. The men playing checkers bend over the board and ponder their moves. A farmer hunkers in the courthouse hallway. And the cedar shavings continue to grow.

Broadus Davidson, freezer foreman, James Jones Slaughterhouse

84

Nashville

How do you take the measure of Nashville? By calling it the mecca for those with musical or political or educational or financial ambitions—a lodestone tugging from the center of the state. It is that. They come to its colleges and universities to earn degrees and launch careers. They follow their campaign slogans and billboard dreams to the steps of the great marble capitol on the hill. They come to its rich, glass-sheathed business district to make it in banking and publishing and insurance. And they come with empty bellies and one-way tickets and guitars slung across their backs to peddle songs that can turn an unknown into the hottest property in town.

87

They come to a town grown sophisticated while exporting country music to the world. The songs were first sung a cappella before the fiddle and, later, guitar and banjo were added as accompaniment. The music lent a festive touch to a life of long working hours. In the 1920s, record companies discovered this very personal form of music and began making forays into Tennessee to record southern musicians.

At the same time, National Life and Accident Insurance Company of Nashville, seeking an advertising outlet, purchased a clear channel 50,000-watt radio station and gave it the call letters, WSM, after the company's slogan, "We Shield Millions." On November 28, 1925, the station manager, George D. Hay, asked a white-bearded fiddler named Uncle Jimmy Thompson to play before the WSM microphone. Afterward, phone calls and telegrams flooded the station, a clear sign country music had a following. Hay later pinned the name *Grand Ole Opry* on a station-sponsored jamboree of country music. By 1939, the Opry was carried nationally by the NBC network.

Various styles influenced country music. In the 1930s, western swing brought drums and amplified instruments to the Opry stage. The popular Hank Williams added a honky-tonk element to the music, and singers Eddy Arnold and Tennessee Ernie Ford helped merge country and popular music. Chet Atkins gave country music greater polish. Bluegrass, meanwhile, returned to the older folk songs but introduced breakneck tempos on the banjo.

Towers of St. Mary's Catholic Church and the State Capitol

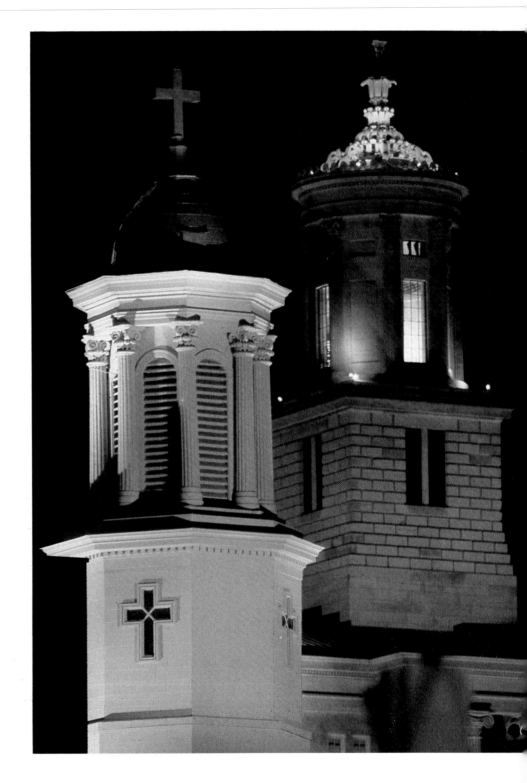

Deadrick Street with War Memorial building

For years, Opry music came from Ryman Auditorium, a thirty-three-hundred-seat fire hazard where entertainers performed on a sweltering stage and where fans crowded around the footlights with their flash-popping cameras. In 1974, the Opry moved to its new $12 million house in an amusement park on the outskirts of Nashville. The family-oriented park is far removed from the beer joints near Ryman Auditorium—an atmosphere more closely attuned to the broken dreams country music speaks to.

Red Lane, songwriter

"Daily you hear the stories of somebody about to give up and they write this little song and they sell eight million records and suddenly they're famous and rich."
—Tom T. Hall on TV talk show

Church Street musician

91

Friedman's Pawn Shop, lower Broadway

Nashville developed a reputation for a unique recording style featuring excellent sidemen, who could not read a note of music, and an atmosphere of intense mutual cooperation. Despite the phenomenal growth of the country music industry in Nashville, this style of recording still exists. So does the belief that the next person who walks into a studio with a crumpled sheet of music in his pocket might have a hit.

Overnight success. It still happens in Nashville, enough to keep you believing. A young skinny kid comes into town to play a gig at the Exit/In and has to plead a twenty-dollar advance to get his equipment to the club. The show begins, and he emerges in a sequined jumpsuit playing a Jimmy Hendrix tribute. His music builds until he is firing hot salvos of notes that bend and shudder and screech in an apocalyptic wail. The sound enters and hums behind the listener's breastbone. The young crowd is on its feet, rolling against him, pulled by his raw force, and the In can't hold it. Tethered by a long cord to his speakers, he walks out the door to the street to play his crashing sound to the mob that follows him. Welcome to the land of infinite possibilities.

Todd Burnett of Jamestown, Tennessee State Fair

Tennessee State Fair

Lower Broadway

Barbara Mandrell   *Loretta Lynn*   *Dolly Parton*

Q: *"How many hours a week does he work?"*
A: *"He might work twenty-four hours a day and then might not work for six months."*
Q: *"How many live in the house?"*
A: *"Five or six or seven depending on who's in town and who's on the road."*
Q: *"How many years of education does the head of the household have?"*
A: *"I see you don't have a box for third grade."*
—Census taker interviewing songwriter's wife

Roy Acuff

Bill Golden, Oak Ridge Boys

Johnny Cash

Minnie Pearl, backstage at the Opry

Fan Fair

Nashville is known as the "Athens of the South" for its replica of the Parthenon and its concentration of colleges and universities. Many of the schools are private, founded through the largesse of individuals or religious denominations. The earliest settlers were literate, but public-supported education did not arrive until after the Civil War. Though the state has a large system of primary and secondary schools, as well as junior colleges and colleges and the University of Tennessee network of campuses, many Tennesseans still elevate "common sense" over "book sense."

At Vanderbilt they teach southern literature with a possessive love. For their own, Robert Penn Warren, John Crowe Ransom, and others, helped fill the course books with a rare poetry and prose. By some design or pure luck, those remarkable writers and poets called The Fugitives gathered in dormitories and Nashville homes in the 1920s and held the attention of the world.

Fifth and Union

96

Fifty years earlier at a black university across town, a handful of singers also drew world acclaim with their beautiful, haunting songs. They were the toast of continents, and their music saved the school from bankruptcy. Now a mural of the original Jubilee Singers is a backdrop in a table-filled room of recruiters from Yale and New York University and the University of North Carolina. They talk with Fisk students about graduate school, and they are all here only because the singers were here first.

Nashville is a center for a number of religious denominations and their publishing arms. It is a city of churches where ministers, like merchants and musicians, tell their own success stories. When Dr. Ira North came to Nashville twenty-nine years ago, he preached to a small group in a basement church. Today, that congregation is the largest Church of Christ in the world. Three times each Sunday, worshipers fill the three-thousand-seat auditorium built over the old basement sanctuary. The church's great outreach program benefits the needy, from homeless children to the elderly. Dr. North knew that Nashville, with its great Bible publishing houses and denominational colleges and church headquarters, was the most fertile ground to plant his ministry. "Nashville, Tennessee," he proclaims with admitted bias, "with all its shortcomings—and they are legion—and with all its faults—and they are many—is the greatest city on earth."

Flag raising atop State Capitol

97

One Commerce Place

"You're so tall, you men,
You Tennesseans. I've never seen so many
tall fellows riding in elevators.
What makes you then so tall? Is it the cornbread
and the buttermilk, or is it in the air,
or is it having to climb so many hills
that makes you stretch your legs?"
Why since you ask,
Tallness is not what you eat or drink
But in the seed of man.
—Donald Davidson, The Tall Men

State Capitol

Roller skaters at the Legislative Plaza

Willard Perdue, shoemaker, Arcade

Bob Lee, rose peddler

Victor Davis, Arcade

Want a Nashville success story? Then visit the portly good ole boy with the pinstripe suit and beard and hamburg. Wayne Oldham crosses his legs on a desk top and grins his squint-eyed grin and tells how he came to Nashville five years back with a franchise in his pocket and little else. Well, he rented a little hole-in-the-wall office on a dead-end street and by himself began putting together a fast-food chain across Middle Tennessee. Now he's got 2,500 employees and a $26 million business. "Yes, sir, there's money in Nashville and its downtown is starting to happen and its moving on like Atlanta and, well, I'd be doggone crazy not to like Nashville, it's been so good to me."

The Arcade

100

Michael Penny, Church Street

The guests arrive in Cadillacs and wear minks—not what you'd expect of people who come to hear some pickin' and singin'. But country music has gone chic, and when they hand out the annual awards, there's a lot of Hollywood mixed in with backwoods Tennessee. Still, the country is there. You see it in the looseness before showtime, in the fun of performing. They wear satin tights and tuxedos, but those are still the faces of dirt farmers' daughters and cotton pickers' sons. They are people who paid stiff dues for their success. The glitter of the new Opry House and the international audience for their music is a testimonial to their art form, one that would not be kept in the coves and hollows. Like the Opry, Nashville is a mixture of gloss and earthiness. Hard-luck Tennessee with its hard-faced girls and honky-tonks laps at the city's wealthy downtown district. Here they come to savor the best of both Nashville worlds—the cotillions and hoedowns.

103

Balloon race from Centennial Park

Franklin

Margaret Wyatt is the most unreconstructed of Southerners. Her Confederate flag flies every day above the door of venerable Wyatt Hall. She holds up for inspection unexploded cannonballs, heavy as shot puts, and boxes of minie balls. She keeps on a shelf a stack of Confederate bills and the wrinkled military pass her grandfather carried from Nashville to Gallatin. She slides from beneath a table the surgical chest carried by Dr. Watson Gentry who amputated General John Hood's leg at the Battle of Chickamauga. She guards cousin Jimmy Cooper's journal detailing the last bloody days of the war. She's never forgiven cousin Jimmy's daughter for marrying "a damned Yankee." Raised on tales told by old veterans, living on ground hallowed by their blood, the war still rages in her breast.

105

Franklin's maple-canopied streets are shadowed by war, for many of its homes can recall one of the most tragic episodes in America's history. At Harrison House, south of town, General John Bell Hood issued the order on November 30, 1864, that sent his tattered Army of Tennessee into what was to become the bloodiest two hours of fighting in American military history—the Battle of Franklin.

The Carter House on Columbia Pike was the center of the Union line and received the brunt of the battle's fury. Today its outbuildings carry more bullet holes and battle scars than any other American structure. It was a few yards from here that young Captain Todd Carter, fighting for the Confederacy, was mortally wounded trying to reach his boyhood home he had not seen for nearly four years. That night, in the wake of the battle, the Carter family found Todd lying in the dark among the dead and dying who were the wreckage of Hood's army. By lantern light they carried him home where he died under the roof where he was born.

Truett Place, white-pillared and proud, standing across the Harpeth River from town, was the command post of Union General John Schofield. On the south balcony of this home, Edwin Truett sought a glimpse of the battle through the field glasses of the officers assembled there. It was General Schofield himself who handed over his binoculars to the boy, saying there would never again be an opportunity to witness such a magnificent spectacle.

The day of the battle was bright and warm. Squirrels and rabbits were flushed from the high grass as the Southern troops advanced. Sunlight glinted from thousands of bayonets and musical instruments as the bright battle colors were unfurled. The last great charge in the western theater of the Civil War had begun.

Candlelight Tour

Main Street

Battle-scarred plantation office of Carter House

Monument to Tennesseans killed at Battle of Franklin

> *"All a person needs in life is the Bible and a copy of* Gone With the Wind.*"*
> —Margaret Wyatt

The calm and stately appearance of Franklin's antebellum homes belies the carnage of that November afternoon more than a hundred years ago. Boxmere, Magnolia Hall, Myles Manor, and others were commandeered as barracks and hospitals for wounded and dying soldiers.

Carnton, built on the Harpeth in the 1820s by Randall McGavock and his wife, was visited often by their friends, Andrew and Rachel Jackson. In the spring of 1861 it had been a parade ground for the mustering of Franklin's young men into the Army of Tennessee. Three years later, as that army dashed its last hopes and strength against the Union line, Carnton's oaken floors were soaked with the blood of neighbors' children. Stretched out on the veranda were the bodies of five of the South's ablest generals: Pat Cleburne, H. B. Granbury, O. F. Strahl, John Adams, and "States Rights" Gist. Today, at the rear of the house, two acres of unassuming stone markers comprise the modest Confederate cemetery where fifteen hundred casualties of the fight were laid to rest.

110

Albert Gordon and son-in-law, Doyle Sullivan

Out of the earth that covers me, a pall
Flung by anonymous hands of men, I cry:
Not in vain, O states,
Not in vain, the blood!

—Donald Davidson, *The Tall Men*

Professor Bob Womack is touched by the rows of un-marked graves. The generals don't interest him much. They are well-buried beneath monuments and their names live on, at least as historical footnotes. But the foot soldiers who slogged their way hundreds of miles, often ill-clad and ill-fed, to preserve an aristocracy of planters, interest him. He resurrects these unknown soldiers through letters and bits of diaries found in basements and attics. The generals wrote for posterity, but these forgotten enlisted men wrote the un-adorned truth of their feelings. Those feelings move Profes-sor Womack to visit the simple graves of these men and leave flowers in their honor.

It seems odd that the Battle of Franklin, one of the most ferocious of the Civil War, should leave behind hardly a military marker. The cannons, pyramids of black cannon-balls, and plaques that pepper other battlefields are seldom seen. But people here don't need stone reminders. Relatives limped wounded from the battle. Generals fell at their back door.

112

Walking Horse Country

7:00 A.M. Sammy Day works Mountain Man for fifteen minutes behind Continental Farms' stable. One more flat pad is added to the hoof. Sammy declares the big stallion "dead on the money."

Set among the wooded knobs and white-fenced pastures of Bedford County are genteel farmhouses with weathered barns and silver-domed silos. When it rains, sheep and cattle graze placidly outdoors to the electric sing of crickets in the bluegrass and the steady drum roll of drizzle on rooftops. But inside clean, airy, cathedral-roofed stables, horses wearing blankets and leg wrappings munch their sweet meal in straw-covered stalls.

115

This is the land of Midnight Sun, Merry Go Boy, Talk of the Town, and other legendary walking horse champions. This is the rich, green turf around Shelbyville and Columbia, around Murfreesboro, Lewisburg, and Wartrace where a hard-working utility animal evolved into a world famous breed of pleasure horse. Here are the stables where densely muscled bays and sorrels and pitch black stallions shift from the flat walk to the running walk to the canter with smooth, inbred power. Here is where groomed and pampered champions command stud fees of $1,000 and up, where horses sell for a quarter million dollars and more. To the walking horse fan, this is the center of the universe.

Highway 99 near Eagleville

Behind Walking Horse Hotel, Wartrace

Shadow Valley Farms, near Shelbyville

5:30 P.M. Rain begins falling. Sammy's heart sinks. A big horse like Mountain Man needs a firm turf. Instead the World Grand Championship will be decided in the mud.

Bedford County is plastered with welcome signs. Buttons and banners proclaim the start of the annual ten-day National Walking Horse Celebration. So do the crowds. Pope's Cafe on the square in Shelbyville is packed with men and women in Stetsons and straight-legged jeans, a long line of Western boots toeing the counter. Crowds flow through the Celebration grounds; people whittling on cedar sticks amble up to admire the play of muscles and velvety sheen of hot and lathered horseflesh. They bunch up at the workout ring where knife traders banter and owners stand quietly beside horses up for sale. It has the tang of a county fair, but there is nothing small time about this event. A couple with mud on their boots climb into their Rolls-Royce to sip champagne.

Begun in 1939, the Celebration is a showcase for a breed touted for its intelligence, gentleness, and extremely smooth gait. "A good one, man, it's better than riding in a Lincoln Continental," says a trainer from West Tennessee. "He's just floating along."

World Grand Champion Class—The Celebration

118

11:00 P.M. A roar goes up as Sammy, riding Mountain Man, enters the ring for the grand championship class. The horse is right, *thinks Sammy,* but can he stay that way?

Even with a steady rain and the track a muddy mess, excitement at the championship is feverish. Women with expensive hairdos and gold earrings stoically accept the gobs of mud kicked on them by horses cantering by the boxes. Men trade jibes. People in the stands surge forward. Soon, everyone is on their feet, yelling and stomping and applauding each time their favorite passes. Wave after wave of screams and cheers break across the stands. Mountain Man is among three finalists, and the judges in rubber boots and slickers have picked the winner. The stadium lights are cut, and a spotlight plays over the field. It sweeps Mountain Man's heaving flank, catches his clouds of breath shot through with rain. Sammy's taut face flashes a second in the blinding light. For one impossibly long, aching moment, the world teeters as the number of the winning horse is slowly read.

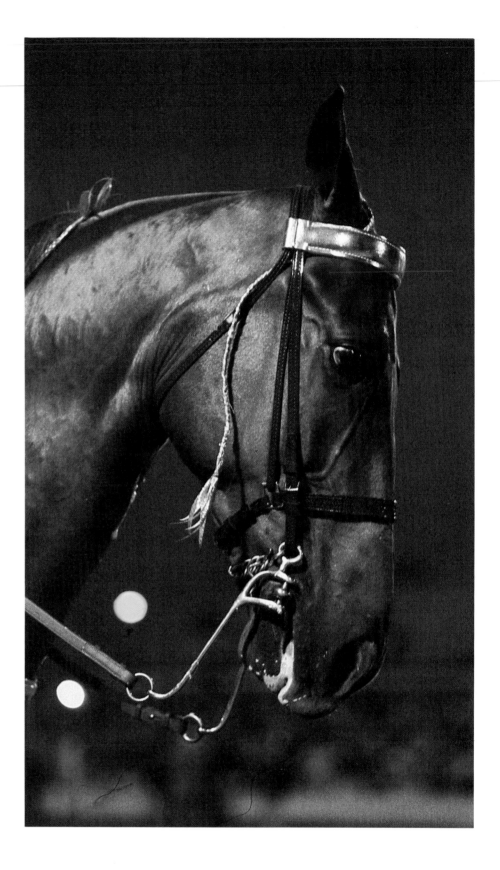

In the ring

120

"These trainers know exactly what they're doing. They have a million dollars tied up in their hands and the seat of their britches."
—Spectator at National Walking Horse Celebration

Continental Farms, Wartrace Road

After midnight. Judy, Sammy's wife, cries over Mountain Man's third-place finish. Nine cases of victory champagne and a tap of beer stand untouched. Flowers and congratulatory telegrams deepen the hurt.

Shelbyville is back to normal. You can find a seat in Pope's Cafe. At their stables, trainers put horses through workouts as strenuous as a day in harness. At Continental Farms, Sammy still grieves over the muddy finals. This was the year Mountain Man was to take it all. A letter arrives from a young fan who won't accept the judges' verdict.

"I still think Mountain Man won it," writes the lad, and Sammy breaks into a broad grin as he shows the letter to the grooms. "He's still my horse. He's the greatest."

The boy's faith is well placed. A year later on a dry track with the crowd surging forward and Sammy up, Mountain Man wins it all.

Stable, The Celebration grounds

"A walking horse will put out more in thirty minutes of practice than a horse plowing all day."
—Trainer Ray Gilmer, Eads, Tennessee

The Amish

Chris Gingerich has the bright, innocent eyes and angelic face of Amish children. His pants are hitched with suspenders, and his forehead, beneath the broad-brimmed felt hat, is framed in gold bangs. When his father, Danny, sings out in Pennsylvania Dutch, "Krislich, kom," Chris comes running to help his father move ancient pieces of equipment, buggies and carts and horse-drawn discs. Chris is only seven years old but work-wise. His small hands are needed on a farm where the simple ways are blessed and machinery is shunned—no trucks or tractors, no televisions, radios, or telephones, no running water or electricity.

Chris's older brother Eli rides the plow behind three broad-rumped Belgians, neatly slicing the earth and turning it up in rich brown furrows. While Chris forks sweet hay to the towering draft horses in the barn or pumps a squeaking gush of water into the trough, his mother and seven sisters scurry about their household chores, the screen door slapping at the austere white farmhouse on the flat Lawrence County plain.

All Amish photographs, Ethridge community, Lawrence County

"If you never had a radio, TV, or car, you don't miss it. And if you don't miss it, you're not tempted by it."
—Amish man

The clang of the dinner bell reaches the field. Danny, Eli, and Chris leave their muddy boots on the porch and wash inside at shallow basins. They sit on long benches with the womenfolk who, from mother to infant, are dressed alike in milkmaid frocks and black bonnets and brogans. There is no talk at the table, just the din of spoons as the shyly smiling children fill their bowls with ground beef and deer meat, yams, corn, applesauce, and pears sweetened with sugar.

There is much to do. Beside the wet fields to turn for spring planting and the cattle to feed, there are busy preparations for a wedding. Like most Amish, the Gingeriches are a large family, and their farmhouse will be crammed with guests. From delivering their children, to schooling, to marrying and burying their own, the Amish are a cloistered society yoked to a horse-and-buggy past—a still water in the turbulent flow of twentieth-century American life.

In the dying light of day, Ure Gingerich, the family patriarch, fixes a bolt on his buggy. He was with the first of his sect to settle Lawrence County in the 1940s. The Amish community has grown to well over a thousand, and his own fold includes twenty-one children and one hundred seventy grandchildren. To be self-sufficient the Amish way takes many hands. "How will you English survive in the city?" he asks repeatedly, knowing his simple lifestyle is immune to the economic and emotional ills of the day.

From dawn, when first light strikes the windmill blade, till after dark, work on the Amish farm is unending, often hard but soul satisfying; evening is magical. Dusk is filled with the castanet clack of horses and the Medieval rumble of heavy wagons. Women move through the rooms of the houses in pools of kerosene light. Buggies with small flickering lights on the running boards pass on the dirt roads. Chris of the bright eyes hangs a lantern from a barn rafter to milk a cow, and the patriarch leans back in a rocker, a toothpick in his mouth, secure on his island, wondering how the English will survive.

"The home is the pulse of Amish life. It is the Alpha and Omega, the beginning and the ending of their lives, and the few God-given years between are a symphony of homespun learning and hard work, mixed with impromptu fun and frolic."
—Donald Donlinger, *The Gentle People*

129

The Tennessee River

A thick mist drapes the groves and meadows at Shiloh battlefield. It lacquers the cannonballs stacked in cairns. It shrouds the graves. It splatters the lights of a pickup that lumbers past fishermen's shanties, past the battlefield to a turnoff at the cinderblock tavern called the Rockpile. The predawn is hushed; the morning beer drinkers are three hours from their rounds. The pickup edges down a steep gravel drive to the river's edge where a fisherman steps from the cab, quietly cusses the fog, and squats against an oak to await first light.

131

A buoy bobs soft and faint in the milky dawn. Ready for a go at the catfish, Cotton Bowden pushes his johnboat into the shallows, yanks twice at the starter cord and putters into the channel. He is a small, tough, sinewy man with thick yellow-gold hair and a face as seamed and cracked as parched earth. For a time a steelworker in Chicago and a store manager in Kokomo, he returned years ago to his home on the river and the solitary life he prefers. "Out here," he says testily, "there are no damned clocks to punch."

Here where Cotton is fishing between Pickwick Dam and Savannah, the river is glassy smooth, but the banks are lost in a thicket of fog. He angles across the river, finds the floating jug that marks his first line, and hauls it in by hand. The line ruffles the surface, breaking the mirror.

The Tennessee shatters into a thousand creeks, a handful of rivers: the foam-busting Ocoee and the placid Sequatchie, the Hiwassee, Watauga, and Nolichucky. They begin in the rain-drenched mountains to the east as runoff streams that fuse and flow into the Tennessee.

Other rivers contribute to the Tennessee—the Holston and French Broad, the Powell and Clinch and Little River. Some recall a land rich in game—the Elk, the Pigeon, the Duck. Swollen with spring rains and winter snows, these tributaries rush to the Tennessee, which runs its swerving course from Knoxville into Alabama, and north to Paducah, flowing in most every direction, slicing the state in two but also tying it together.

At the banks of an old community called Forks in the River two miles east of Knoxville, the Holston and French Broad flow together to become the Tennessee. Here begins the river that carried crops out of the mountains and manufactured goods back, that brought settlers down river and invading armies upriver. Its waters were used to brew river coffee and to baptize souls. For centuries it fought every effort by man to tame it, then found itself shackled and subdued in one furious decade of dam building. The Tennessee has been a civilizer and destroyer, a villain and benefactor.

*McKinley Gant, groundskeeper,
Shady Grove Methodist Church near Saltillo*

The river hooks its way through Chattanooga, cutting the same channel John Donelson followed when he led women and children in rafts on the circuitous journey to the new settlement of Nashville. Indians fell on the party's sick, killing the stragglers. Soon afterward, a crude warehouse, ferry, and landing were established—the seed for the embryonic city of Chattanooga.

Chattanooga boasted only twelve hundred inhabitants in 1842 when an advertisement for city lots declared confidently that "the rapid increase of trade and population is almost without parallel . . . and it will no doubt . . . become a large city." The prophecy was accurate. Factors that made its capture so important to Union forces in 1863—its strategic location as a river and rail center—assured it a strong future. Despite periodic floodings, financial panics, and plagues, Chattanooga emerged as a heavy industry town in one of the most naturally beautiful settings in the country. While foundries turn out iron castings, brake drums, pressure vessels, and boilers, tourists by the thousands visit its mountains, battlefields, and lakes.

136

Saltillo ferry

He is the old man of this river. At ninety-six, he is still solid as a steel pier. His lusty laugh bounces off the low ceiling of his home, a houseboat set on concrete blocks on the river bank. For years, Captain O. B. Gladish piloted an excursion boat up and down the river at Chattanooga, and before that he traveled like Huck Finn in a tent aboard a scow, trapping the river to Muscle Shoals. He has seen it all: paddlewheelers riding floodwaters through the downtown streets of the city; the infamous suck at Walden's Gorge, where a whirlpool could grab a boat in the time it took a pilot to brush a fly from his face; the coming of the dams that drowned the dangerous rocks; the coming of the roads and railways that dried up steamboat trade. Through it all the city grew, and on summer evenings the old pilot rocks in his porch chair and looks across the quiet, deep river to the mountains beyond.

Charlie Pipes, ferryman

Cotton Bowden's boat skims past Shiloh, his childhood playground. Here, he dug up scores of minie balls for sinkers and dozens of arrowheads for war games. *Shiloh,* an ancient Hebrew word meaning place of peace, has become a modern byword for bloodbath. But Cotton is locked in a daily struggle with the river, and so for him its history is an aside. Only when he turns the johnboat home at the end of the day is there time to savor the beauty and tranquility of the river. He crosses his legs, leans back against the outboard, and draws on the river's presence. His world grows calm; his leathery face softens. "Mighty peaceful," he says, transfixed by the mist climbing off the water. "Man, it's a beautiful life on the river."

Mallard at Hamburg Bottom

Jackson

A turntable and speakers sit on the edge of the boxing ring, and Jackie Bearden, glistening with sweat, skips to a disco beat. A bell clangs and he stops. Sweat streams down his smooth, unmarked face. A buzzer sounds, and he begins shooting three minutes of cat-quick combinations into the heavy bag. It reels and jerks on its chain. The bell clangs, and now he climbs through the ropes to spar with his brother, Obie. Jackie is teaching, so there is no sting to his punches. He feints, weaves, and slips blows. His arms move like pistons. Time after time, his fists flick at Obie's young, unflinching face. The music pulses through the old gym as the brothers dance and jab. Jackie, you see, is aiming for the Olympics, and one day, he says, Obie will be there too.

141

Clyde and Della Watkins

There is a strong air of organized competitiveness in Jackson. The tennis courts at Muse Park are filled at night; students at a karate academy kick high and yell in unison like a fearsome chorus line; tykes submerged in helmets and shoulder pads run through pass and block drills; high school teams win state titles, little leaguers play in world series, Jackson's golden gloves team is ranked among the nation's best.

Jackson—named after Andrew Jackson—is eight square miles on the Forked Deer River and is the seat of a county named for James Madison. Locals boast that Davy Crockett, an itinerant telegraph worker named Thomas Edison, and author Lew Wallace (who wrote *Ben Hur*) all lived there. General Grant had his Union headquarters on Main Street, and the town suffered under the battles of the Civil War.

Jackson achieved recognition when the railroads came to West Tennessee. It was an age of steam locomotives and

Ervin Flakes

W. F. Norwood and James Rushing, Iselin yards

Going to market, U. S. Highway 70

"When I started on the railroad, I enjoyed taking a train a couple hundred miles down the road. There you were, handling a million dollars worth of motor and no telling how much in freight. You felt part of a big operation. It just seemed an accomplishment one man could move all that from one town to another."

—T. T. Haskins, railroad engineer

143

Jessie Lewis

Casey's body lies buried in Jackson, Tennessee
Close beside the tracks of the old IC.
May his spirit live forever throughout the land,
As the greatest of all heroes of a railroad man.

Casey Jones, he died at the throttle,
Casey Jones, with a whistle in his hand.
Casey Jones, he died at the throttle,
But we'll all see Casey in the promised land.

—"The Ballad of Casey Jones"

St. Luke's Episcopal Church

Summertime, U. S. Highway 70

colorful trains which carried the imagination and cargo to such faraway places as Chicago, Topeka, and New Orleans. Three railroads passed through Jackson, creating a storybook landscape of switchyards, roundhouses, hotels, and neat rows of trainmasters' Victorian homes. These men and their trains created legends larger than life. John Luther Jones became famous through a song about his death in a train wreck, but at the time Casey Jones was just a neighbor in the clapboard house down the street. Sons followed fathers into a lifetime of work at the train shops, and the engineer's wife instinctively recognized the distant sound of a late night whistle announcing her husband's return from a run on the line.

When the city's railroad boom played out in the 1960s, Jackson competed with the same fierce zeal for new industries as it does in sports. And it landed them. Oldtimers who years ago wielded long-nose oil cans and blew steam whistles on locomotives, who worked at Jackson's busy Frogmoor and Iselin railyards and lived near the widow Casey Jones, now see their sons working at sprawling plants set in fields of clipped grass. The railroad is still important to Jackson, to be sure, but the tradition of son following father to the yards is gone.

N. T. Richardson at his Grand Junction general store

Grand Junction– LaGrange

The sun peeks over an aging row of stores, then rises beside a water tower marked GRAND JCT. TENN. A freight rushes out of the morning's silence with a raucous thunder and clack. Rails bend and bolts dance under the weight. The din ends as abruptly as it began. Silence.

A single skylight illumines the cavernous store belonging to N. T. Richardson—the same general merchandise store he has operated the past fifty-four years. That's long enough to have witnessed the surge and ebb of this once-busy railroad junction. Which he has. That's also long enough to develop the reputation of a crusty character. Which he is. N. T. once chased a Memphis photographer from the store, townsfolk say, and they warn about asking the spry old man his age. He was a character witness at a trial when an uninformed lawyer popped that question. "None of your damned business," N. T. shot back, drowning the court in laughter.

Junction of the Southern and the Illinois Central Gulf Railroads

Retired railroad men and farmers in overalls sit on the stoop outside the Richardson store and chew on the past. They glance at the weed-filled railroad lot where rosebushes once bloomed. They talk of the days when passenger and freight trains pulled in every fifteen minutes, when three telegraph operators worked the depot, when Grand Junction lived up to its name.

"Casey Jones was an engineer, that's for sure," says N. T., aiming a squirt of Pen's Natural Leaf tobacco at the roadway in front of the store. As a youngster, he stood at crossings to wave at the legendary conductor highballing freight through Grand Junction to the markets in Chicago. Jones died in 1900. A three-story hotel and depot at Grand Junction was dismantled later in the century, a victim of evaporating passenger service and competition from Memphis, sixty miles to the west. Trains on the intersecting Southern and IC Gulf lines no longer stop here—just a long, flat whistle blast and through.

Woodlawn, headquarters for General Sherman during area Civil War engagements

Magnolia

"Memphis used to be a saloon town, wild and rugged. The nice women of Memphis got on the train and came down here to shop."

—Courtney Parham, LaGrange

Woodlawn

John Walley makes men's cologne inside the old slave quarters behind his antebellum home at LaGrange. He keeps vials and beakers of sweet smelling essences on a cluttered work table, and a huge flask of alcohol under lock in the back. His cologne firm, perhaps the smallest in the world, is named Reverie after his 150-year-old plantation house.

Once, it was the smell of war that drifted through Reverie and the other stately homes at LaGrange. In one house, a planter's steely-nerved wife played the piano while servants hid the silverware. In another, floorboards are still stained with the blood of wounded soldiers bandaged there. The residents of one home were given three rooms to live in while the enemy quartered officers through the rest of the house and privates camped on the grounds.

Three years the occupation lasted. Grant and Sherman stayed for a time, and before it was over, the fine academies were torn down and the church pews turned to coffins for young men from New York, Indiana, and Illinois. A town that surpassed Memphis in wealth and culture was left, by one Union captain's account, "dry and pulseless and black." Reverie and a handful of other fine homes survived.

If you happen by the grounds at Reverie, look out for the peacock and the raccoon and the muzzled dog. And don't say anything about the tombstone in the backyard, an anniversary gift from Walley to his wife Betty. (What made her mad, he says, was putting her birthdate on it.) This is by way of saying the Walleys are exotic and that makes them proper inhabitants of LaGrange. This West Tennessee time capsule is as rare as any fragrance conjured by Walley—a distillate of Doric columns and magnolia bloosoms, big lawns and intricate woodwork, proud matrons who raise an imperious eyebrow when they talk, and newcomers zealous to preserve this token of Old South wealth and culture. La-Grange has lost its prominence but not its aura of good breeding. The homes are named Chantilly and Reverie, Tiara and Serenity; their owners are steeped in the courtesy and calling of the old way.

John Walley, Reverie plantation

John Vickers and bottle tree

152

Malinda Poplar

Willie Robinson

"*I've always said I'd just as soon live in West Tennessee as anywhere in the world, and in Grand Junction if we have waterworks or lights. Now we have both, and I'm just as happy as I can be.*"
—R. B. Pankey, ninety-year-old former train mailman

O. C. Poplar

Fayette County

Houston, Texas . . . Baton Rouge, Louisiana . . . Memphis, Tennessee. Marion Parham calls out the names of towns stamped on the bottom of Coke bottles with the excited ring of a croupier at a high-stakes roulette wheel. Newton, Mississippi. "Boy, you're just twiddling your thumbs," he wisecracks as he hands a bottle to a loser. Miami, Florida . . . Boston, Massachusetts. This last bottle is his. "A sho-nuff winner," he chirps.

Parham and the other well-to-do landowners huddled around the counter pull out a U. S. map with one end of a cloth ruler tacked to where Fayette County ought to be. They peer at the ruler and pull it tight. Boston is farther than Miami, sure enough. "Thank you, boys," says Parham, his eyes twinkling, as he pockets $1.25, the spoils of a game of "faraway bottle."

Square Morman's homeplace

O. D. Maclin, near Somerville

"When everything is going well, I stand in the middle of those crops and feel joy."
—O. D. Maclin

Square Morman, Rossville

Alberta Perry and great-grandson, Eric

By the measure of lifestyles, Fayette County is equally distant from all big cities. People on their porches wave at strangers. Tools are unlocked and keys are left in tractors. Old homeplaces stand vacant for years without a broken window. Whose garden yields more crop is a topic of friendly back porch debate.

Poplar Avenue begins at Moscow in south Fayette County, but the open land, the morning quiet, the dirt roads feeding into Poplar belie the fact that this is the beginning of a mighty thoroughfare into the pounding heart of Memphis.

*"We're just passing by for a few days in this life.
So you learn to be helpful to your brother.
Brothers don't have no color."*

—The gospel of life according to O. D. Maclin

Follow a winding dirt road in Fayette County. Along the river bottoms and gentle slopes, in the flats and folds of the land, cash is ripening in rows as far as the eye can see: billowy seas of soybeans, acres of cotton plants and tall ears of corn, cattle in the pasture, quail in an orchard, and a doe on the edge of a field.

Summer yields its traditional bounty in Fayette County, but the means of taking it have changed. Gone are the mules. Gone is the man with his wife and children bending over rows of cotton, picking the bolls by hand. Gone or almost gone are the tenant farmers, black people who worked on shares and signed their names with an "X." Gone is the music of the field hands. In the middle of the county, a successful black farmer now sits in his glassed-in tractor cab, safe from bee stings, comforted by air conditioning, soothed by stereo.

But the farmer in Fayette County is never really safe. He is always a worried man. A sudden drought can parch his green crop. Or the rains may come daily, with the fury of coastal squalls, lashing the soybean and cotton plants, choking the fields with weeds. A day starts blue and bright and suddenly turns dark and ominous. A white stallion races the wind for cover. A crop-duster pilot in a baling-wire plane ("Instruments? What for? I got no time to look at them.") is driven from the skies. The fungicide waits. So does the farmer.

The harvest is year-round in the coffee-colored Wolf River. An old, gaunt, round-shouldered man checks his trotline at dawn. Around a bow of the river, a young man wearing a deer hunter's cap squats to his neck in the cold swamp water. He feels for the sunken log and, finding it, holds the open end tightly to his chest. When the spawning fish tries to dart free, the young fisherman will grab it and beach it in his johnboat. In an era of combines and crop dusters, grabbling for fish is as ancient as the Indians. The young fisherman learned it from his trapper father.

159

Pick up the dirt road again where the buildings begin: A cinder-block beer joint where men lounge out front in the dusk; a Pentecostal church where a woman in a white dress holds her palms to heaven and shakes, filled with the spirit of revival; a ramshackle house where a woman washes Mason jars in a pan of sudsy brown water that her young grandson drew from the well.

Look for the home with the billy goats and the outhouse and the junked cars and the man whose laughter soars like a child's. Square Mormon is an exuberant, barrel-chested man with a gap-toothed grin. His eyes dance when he talks about the Poor People's Health Clinic he founded at Rossville, no small feat for a man with just a grade school education. "We were in a no-man's-land for medical service," he says. Nine of his ten children have left the county, meanwhile, with little choice but to seek better jobs in big cities. But he stays. He has his mission. And in the evening when the gold light throws long shadows across his farm, he puts his big arms around his grandsons, showing them how to swing a bat, his boyish laughter rising higher than their own.

160

Lynwood Ondrusek, clipping the teeth of newborn piglets, Bill Cowen's farm

Willie Nathan, peach picker

Jay, Lillian, Landra, and Larry Reed,
Highway 57 near Rossville

161

Memphis

At the turn of the century, W. C. Handy searched hard for a lyric to express the raucous vitality of Beale Street in Memphis. The cobblestone street lined with shops, theaters, bars, and casinos catered to blacks and adventuresome whites who attended "Midnight Ramble," an all-black musical review on Thursday nights. Someone joked that the only thing to close down Beale Street at night was a shooting, and Handy finally had his verse. He ran to his office above P. Wee's Saloon and wrote, "You'll find that business never closes till somebody gets killed."

Indeed, there is something exciting and adventurous about Memphis. It is a treasure of Deep South lore, a rich mosaic of king cotton, old man river, and birth of the blues. The legends and legacies of Memphis all begin on the river; paddlewheelers shouldered each other at their moorings on the sloping rock wharf; Beale Street ran east from the river with a raw turn-of-the-century energy that burst into the blues; at brokerage houses on Front Street, men stood beneath skylights to grade the white gold of the Delta.

163

Sunrise from Arkansas shore

Harahan Bridge, circa 1917

On the riverfront today, the aroma of diesel floats on the water, and light dances on the hulls of boats like wisps of smoke. A bearded towboat pilot stares out the wrap-around glass of the bridge, pushing ahead of him three acres of barges filled with ketones and acids. The powerful boat grinds slowly north against the hard current. Rock dikes have corseted the river, creating faster channels than when Mark Twain's paddlewheelers churned up the Mississippi. Viewed from the bluffs or bridges, the Mississippi doesn't roll along—it whirls and boils by Memphis.

Illinois Central Gulf Railroad at Noconnah Creek

Cotton Exchange, Front Street

165

Memphis was created in 1819 by three Nashville real estate developers, one of whom was Andrew Jackson. The city was captured early in the Civil War, but it suffered less in captivity than from three yellow fever epidemics that killed thousands of residents in the 1870s and sent thousands more scurrying for a healthier climate. With just a small segment of the population staying on to care for the sick and bury the dead, the city temporarily went out of existence in 1879.

But neither war nor pestilence could kill Memphis. The population exploded at the turn of the twentieth century, and Memphis became one of the world's great cotton centers. It also became a distribution center for the Mid-South, shipping more hardwood than any other U. S. port. Ornately decorated buildings testified to the wealth of the city. Memphis offered fine hotels for the planters in from the country and famous Beale Street as a magnet for black workers from the Delta. Memphis became a great melting pot of rich and poor, black and white—a city that offered fine fashions and voodoo potions.

Two men came from Mississippi to Memphis where they rose to positions of immense influence. Edward Crump became the "boss" of Memphis, a man with enough political power to handpick Tennessee governors and congressmen for decades. Elvis Presley moved with his parents to a cold-water flat on Poplar Avenue. When the international recording star died at his mansion in Memphis in 1978, tens of thousands of fans in an outpouring of grief made the pilgrimage to honor the "king of rock 'n roll."

Hernando DeSoto Bridge

Dressed for the muggy summer heat in open knit shirts and bright colored slacks, merchants gather each morning at the revolving doors of the prestigious Cotton Exchange on Front Street. The biggest cotton production has moved to the giant spreads of the West, away from the rich alluvial soil of the Mississippi Valley, but Memphis remains the largest spot-cotton market in the world. The fraternity of Memphis brokers trades six million bales a year without written contract. A man's word is still his bond. Inside the nineteenth-century brokerage buildings near the riverfront, men peel through tagged samples of cotton at long rows of tables. The floor becomes littered with discards that are swept out a door.

Mural "Mississippi at Memphis,"
old Lawrence Furniture Company building

While the river is a link with the past, while the city wears an Old South patina, there is also a new Memphis growing out in concentric circles from the core. Here is a city of vast plants for the processing or distribution of cotton and lumber and cattle. Here is a land of high-rise offices, wood and stone apartments, swank specialty shops, and tree-screened homes. And from the heart of downtown there are other sounds besides the blues. On Mid-America Mall, a gregarious sailor on leave from his boat hawks dress belts draped over his shoulder in a rainbow of leather strips. "Honey, I've got any color you want," he jives. "Just lighten my load." A broadly grinning fellow with an orange afro, a feather stuck in the back of his hair, tells jokes to passersby for his own amusement. A black evangelist in a baggy gray suit and straw hat paces down the mall preaching from a Bible held flush to his face. Sweat streams down his cheeks. "We live in a dangerous time in the last days," he rails.

I'm goin' down the river, goin' down to the river,
  goin' to take my rockin chair,
Goin' to the river, goin' to take my rockin' chair
Blues overtake me goin' to rock away from here.
Oh de Mississippi River, Mississippi River so deep
  an' wide,
I said the Mississippi River's so deep and wide.
Man I love, he is on the other side.
—W. C. Handy, "The Memphis Blues"

Hernando DeSoto Bridge

169

Ma Rainey swathes her bulk in a pink chiffon dress and pink slippers. Her lower lip juts out as she leans back in her chair on the stage at Blues Alley on Front Street and gyrates her hips to the music. She is seventy-two. "I can't cut the mustard," she says in her husky voice, taking a long, hard, wicked look at the audience, then grins, "but I still like to lick the jar." Ma Rainey and "Slopjar" Laury and Big Sam and Sonny "Harmonica" Blake and other blues singers perform a litany of songs and jokes for the faithful who come to Memphis. During the years Beale Street lay fallow, they kept the music alive at home and abroad. It translates to any language. Says Sonny, who left driving a tractor for the harmonica, "A guy is telling the true story of his life when he sings the blues."

Beale Street graffiti

Little Laura Dukes, Blues Alley

"You don't learn the blues in school. They ain't got it wrote in no book. There ain't no seminary for the blues. You inherit the blues. It's born in you. Blues is the voice of the soul."

—Blues singer and pianist, Memphis

Rudy "Summertime" Williams, Blues Alley

If the city begins on the river, it ends here too. Families, lovers, photographers are drawn like lemmings to the water-front. The sun sets on the city and the state with a fireball brilliance that rivals in spectacle the purple mountains of East Tennessee and the rich green dales in the central state. Still high enough to be buttery yellow, the sun nests in the arching lace of Hernando DeSoto Bridge. By the time the sun drops behind a screen of trees on the Arkansas bank, it has flared up fire red. Gazers on the bluff turn to go. Then the encore. Colors explode just above the horizon, staining the clouds with pinks and ambers. The colors grow pure and intense. For one symphonic moment, everything else is shut out of mind. There is but beauty to behold.

Graceland, estate of Elvis Presley

Carter's Seed Store, Front Street

*I looked upon the Nile and raised
    the Pyramids above it,
I heard the singing of the Mississippi
    when Abe Lincoln went down to
    New Orleans,
And I've seen its muddy bosom turn
    all golden in the sunset.
I've known rivers;
Ancient, dusky rivers;
My soul has grown deep like
    the rivers.*

—Langston Hughes, from "The Negro Speaks of Rivers"

172

ROBIN HOOD

Governor Lamar Alexander

Lamar Alexander is an eighth-generation East Tennessean who grew up hiking in the Great Smoky Mountains.

His successful campaign to become the forty-fifth Governor of Tennessee in 1978 was based on a six-month, 1,022-mile walk across the state—from Maryville to Mountain City to Memphis. Each day he stopped at schools, factories, fairs, and churches to visit directly with citizens. At night he stayed with families along the way.

As a youngster, Alexander won two statewide piano competitions. During his term as governor, he has performed classical and country pieces at benefit concerts with ten of Tennessee's symphonies and community orchestras.

While at Maryville High School, Alexander was elected Governor of Tennessee "Boys State." He was a Phi Beta Kappa graduate of Vanderbilt University and law review editor at New York University before entering private law practice in Nashville. (He was Senator Howard Baker's first legislative assistant.)

Alexander and his wife, the former Honey Buhler, have four children: Drew, Leslee, Kathryn, and Will.

PEGGY HOOD

Robin Hood

Pulitzer prize winning photographer Robin Hood is currently Director of Photography for the State of Tennessee. He traveled twenty-five thousand miles throughout the state to capture the moods and images which appear in this book.

Hood was awarded the coveted Pulitzer Prize for Feature Photography for his moving image of a double-amputee Vietnam veteran holding his small child at an Armed Forces Day Parade in 1977. At the time he was a staff photographer for the *Chattanooga News-Free Press*.

A native of Chattanooga, Hood attended the University of Chattanooga where he studied art under noted southern painter George Cress. After graduation, he enlisted in the Army, was commissioned Lieutenant, and served in South Vietnam as an information officer.

Hood lives in Franklin with his wife, Peggy, and daughters, Farrar and Nicole.

MICHAEL CRAWFORD

Barry Parker

Barry Parker is Director of Community Relations at Hamilton Memorial Hospital in Dalton, Georgia, where his communications projects have won statewide awards.

He has traveled throughout Europe, worked on an Israeli kibbutz, and hiked a major portion of the Appalachian Trail, including the mountains of Tennessee.

Parker, a native of Chattanooga, received his B.A. degree in English from Vanderbilt University. After graduation, he worked for United Press International in Alabama and Mississippi and covered a wide range of stories from sports to the civil rights movement. He also served as a legislative writer and a bureau manager. Later, he wrote news and feature articles for the Raleigh (North Carolina) *News and Observer* and the *Chattanooga News-Free Press*.

Parker lives with his wife, LeNét, and son, Adam, on Missionary Ridge in Chattanooga.

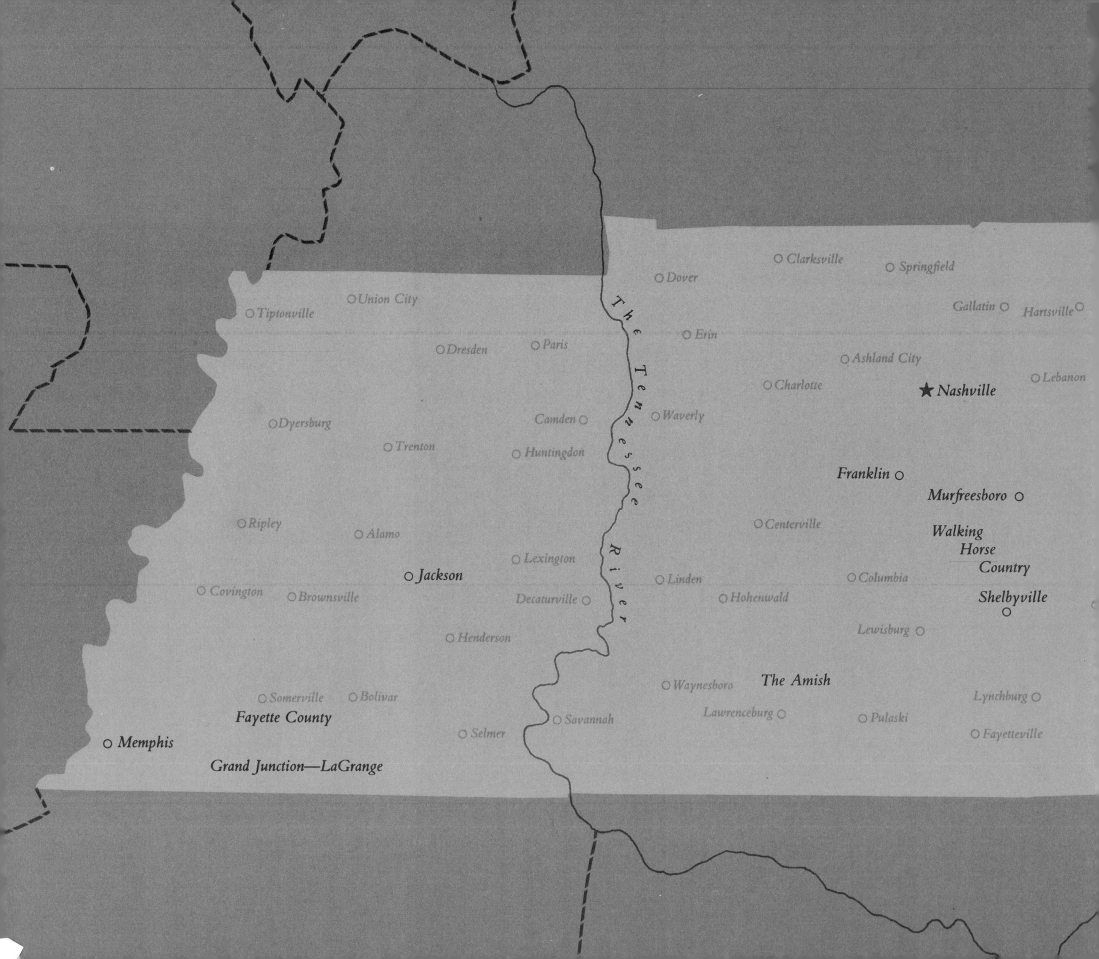